UNEXPECTED TREASURES

72 WAYS TO UNCOVER YOUR HIDDEN WEALTH

Finding Wealth in Life Where You Never Thought to Look

DR. MIKEL BROWN

Copyrighted Material

Unexpected Treasures

CJC PUBLISHING COMPANY

1208 Sumac Dr
El Paso, TX 79925

Copyright © 2010 by CJC Publishing Company
Printed in the United States of America
Library of Congress Control Number: 2010923643
ISBN: 978-1-930388-28-4

Editorial Assistance for CJC Publishing Co by: Delgar Publishing

Cover and Interior design by: 1106 Design

For information about this title or to order other books and/or electronic media, contact the publisher:
www.CJCPublishing.com
(915) 595-1307

All scripture is quoted from the The Living Bible and the The New King James Version of the Bible unless otherwise noted.

ALL RIGHTS RESERVED

No part of this publication may be reproduced, stored in a retrieval system, or transmitted in any form or by any means, electronic, mechanical, photocopying, recording, scanning, or otherwise, except as permitted under Section 107 or 108 of the 1976 United States Copyright Act, without either the prior written permission of the Publisher. Requests to the Publisher for permission should be addressed to the Permissions Department, CJC Publishing, 1208 Sumac Drive, El Paso, TX 79925, 915-595-1307, fax 915-595-1493, e-mail: permcoordinator@cjcpublishing.com.

Publisher's Cataloging-in-Publication
(Provided by Quality Books, Inc.)

Brown, Mikel.
   Unexpected treasures : 72 ways to uncover your hidden wealth / M. Abe Brown.
   p. cm.
   Includes index.
   ISBN-13: 978-1-930388-28-4
   ISBN-10: 1-930388-28-4

   1. Success—Psychological aspects.   I. Title.

BF637.S8B76 2010   158.1
                          QBI10-899

Dedication

To my wife, Deb, who makes me feel as if I won a championship when she married me. To my children, Kelle, Quita, Junior, Josh, Kyla and Matt and all my grandchildren, my legacy is for you.

To my mother, Arleen, and four brothers, Kenny, Tony, Corrie and Big D. (Darrol)

◆ ◆ ◆

In loving memory of Jeffroe Brown, Jr., my beloved brother and encourager. I miss you! You have always celebrated my accomplishments and made me feel exceptional.

◆ ◆ ◆

Special thanks to my Platinum Millionaire Connection Associates:

Scott Whittle
Tish Times
Stacy Horton
Charles Bennett
Willie Jenkins
Laura Whittle
William "Bill" Smith
Lyndon Mayfield

And to the countless others who support my dream.

Table of Contents

Introduction		ix
1	No Knees, No Elbows and No Excuses	1
2	Maintaining Mental Toughness in Tough Times	5
3	The Number One Excuse Is….	9
4	The Rhythm of Life	11
5	Valuable Lessons for Success	13
6	My Protégé's Mistake	15
7	Develop Your Full Potential	17
8	Avoiding Seven Destructive Financial Patterns	21
9	Does Your Paycheck Reflect Your Self-Esteem?	25
10	You Can Do It! It's Not Too Late	29
11	A Simple Twist to Upgrade Your Money Potential	33
12	Turbocharge Your Life	37
13	The Quiet Character of a Strong Woman	41
14	Making This Year Your Best Year Yet!	47
15	Understanding the Power of Endurance	51
16	A Good Person Cannot Be Kept Down	53
17	May the Force Be with You	55
18	Tenacity is a Developed Attribute	57
19	I Fought Three Tough Guys and Won	61
20	The One Mistake Most People Make	63
21	Procrastination: The Enemy of Success	65
22	Would You Stand Out in a Group of 100 People?	69
23	Five Great Lessons From a Pencil	73

24	Living with the Fear of Challenge	77
25	You Are Incredible	79
26	Education Does Not Guarantee Success	83
27	The Death of Dysfunction	85
28	Is Your Life Good?	89
29	Take Control of Your Life!	91
30	Getting Out of Debt? Hogwash	93
31	Hidden Money	95
32	Achieving Success without Regret	97
33	Watch Your Attitude	99
34	Understanding Yourself	101
35	The Secrets to Success	103
36	World Shaper or Moneymaker?	105
37	Discover Your Passion	109
38	Legacy! What is Yours?	111
39	There is a Champion in You	113
40	The Rule of First Things First	117
41	Back from Divorce	121
42	A Simple Solution for Simple Problems	125
43	Overcoming Opposition	127
44	The Secret to Perseverance	131
45	Divorce Statistics and What They Mean to You	133
46	Seven Steps to Enjoy Your Life	135
47	Who is Cheating You?	137
48	The Dream Provides the Means	139
49	Want More, Learn More	141
50	How to Fine-Tune Your Mentality	143
51	A Premier Life Principle	145
52	Don't Drop Your Day Job to Begin Living Your Dreams	147
53	Believe What You Know	149
54	Essentials for Reaching the Top: Principles for Staying There	151

Table of Contents

55	What Motivates You?	153
56	Real Teamwork	155
57	Reaching Your Dream Destination	157
58	I Thought Like a Champion, but I Couldn't Fight a Lick	159
59	Can You Handle the Truth?	163
60	Change is Inevitable	165
61	Navigational Principles in a Bad Economy	167
62	What is Leasing Space in Your Head?	171
63	Six Awesome Points for Greatness	173
64	Awakening the Seed of Potential	177
65	The Value of Experience	179
66	Excuse Me, Can I Order Success Here?	183
67	Living By Your Convictions	187
68	I Planted Corn, but I Expected Wheat	191
69	I Thought I Was in Hawaii…	195
70	They Said Walt Disney Had No Imagination	199
71	Turning Stress Into Strength	203
72	The Power of NOW	207
About The Author		211
Index		213

Introduction

YOU ARE SUDDENLY FACED with divorce papers, or you went to work and received a layoff notice without any indication that it was coming, or you are informed by your doctor that a small mass was discovered during a routine examination; you are now filled with anxiety and questions rather than answers. During times like these, our first inclination is to lean toward the negatives instead of seeking out the positives. We have a tendency to allow the present situation to dictate a feeling of desperation, instead of using it to motivate a constant search for inspiration.

Dr. Mikel Brown has counseled and mentored many people from rocky marriages to rocketing careers, and have found one common trend among all of them. And that is that people rarely have answers, but they can ask hundreds of questions. While it is not wrong to have questions, it is a matter of the kind of questions you are scanning your information base to ask. If you are asking questions such as, "Why is this happening to me," your questions are coming from the mindset of that of a victim. What kind of answer do you expect from a question like this? How would you react if your answer were, "Because you are a bad, inconsiderate, and selfish person and you deserve all of these bad things and more?" The truth of the matter is that asking "why" is an injustice to your future. Regardless of what happened—it happened, and you can do something about what should occur next.

I have come to believe that there are no handicaps or disadvantages, just people who believe there are. Time and time again, people with obvious shortcomings have proven that what one person may have over another does not create a disadvantage. The first chapter in this book deals with people such as Kyle Maynard who was born with no elbows and no knees. Kyle became a college award-winning wrestler because he did not see his lack of elbows and knees as a negative.

Your inspiration will always rise from within you if you see your external attacks as opportunities to transform your weaknesses into advantages. Dr. Mikel Brown is among the best in his field. He knows how to move a person and to point them in the direction of their treasures; treasures that lie dormant inside each frail and yet powerful creation. You are your greatest asset and in this book, you will discover why.

No Knees, No Elbows and No Excuses

From the entrepreneur, to the neurosurgeon, to the professional athlete, there is one common trait found in all successful people. That trait is an uncommon belief in one's ability to succeed and persevere beyond unimaginable hardship and setback.

Why waste time attempting to achieve what you do not believe you can achieve? Many people make half-hearted attempts to accomplish things they do not sincerely believe they can. Michael Jordan was, without doubt, the greatest basketball player of all time—not just because he had exceptional talent but because of his indomitable will to win. His greatness went far beyond physical abilities; it extended to a deep-seated passion that enabled him to turn mere talent into unbelievable artistry on the court. Many NBA players possess rare talent; they would not have gotten to that level without it. However, Michael Jordan became great because, at the time,

> Why waste time attempting to achieve what you do not believe you can achieve?

he worked harder than anyone else in the league to turn physical potential into superior ability. The result was that he performed athletic feats that defied everyone else's beliefs but his own. He pushed the limits of possibility by setting high goals and working hard to accomplish them.

Thomas Edison was relentless in his efforts to invent the light bulb—so much so that he failed over 700 times before achieving his objective. His belief that his efforts would one day pay off was so powerful that surrendering to the temptation to quit was never an option he wanted to entertain. Most inventors would never have ventured beyond the 100th misfire, let alone the 700th. However, Thomas Edison was no ordinary inventor. Clearly, he saw something that fueled his passion to push past one disappointment after another. Those individuals who demonstrate an unwavering belief in themselves provide a great deal for us to examine. Namely, they underscore the fact that there are no failures in life, only quitters.

Kyle Maynard is another encouraging example of someone who defies the odds to live out his passions. As the author of the book "No Excuses," Mr. Maynard certainly leaves very little room for anybody to feel good about making excuses for failure. Kyle was born without knees or elbows, and yet he overcame those physical handicaps to become a world-class wrestler. He did not allow perceived disadvantages to stop him from achieving any of his personal goals. How is it possible for Kyle Maynard to accomplish so much with his obvious limitations while others fail to achieve theirs without having any personal handicaps of this magnitude? With most individuals, fear is their only crippling handicap.

Below is a list of a few noteworthy individuals who refused to quit and overcame extreme adversity in order to take their place in history:

- German composer, Ludwig Van Beethoven—was deaf and psychologically impaired.
- American inventor, Thomas Alva Edison, regarded as the "Father of Electricity"—was deaf and had learning disabilities.
- American author and lecturer, Helen Keller—was deaf and blind.

No Knees, No Elbows and No Excuses

- British statesman, soldier, and author, Sir Winston Churchill—had a learning disability and a bipolar disorder. He was Prime Minister of Great Britain during World War II and received the Nobel Prize for literature in 1953.
- German-American theoretical physicist, Albert Einstein—had a learning disability.
- African-American comic and actress, Whoopi Goldberg—has a learning disability. In 1990, she received an Oscar for Best Supporting Actress.
- The thirty-second president of the United States from 1933–1945, Franklin D. Roosevelt—contracted polio in 1921. As a result, he used a wheelchair and wore leg braces.
- African-American track and field sprinter, Wilma Rudolph—was the first American woman to win three gold medals in one Olympic game. At age four, she was stricken with scarlet fever, double pneumonia, and polio, and experienced partial paralysis.
- American actor, James Earl Jones—overcame a bad stutter in college, and he is now famous for his voice role as Darth Vader, in Star Wars.
- Country and Western singer, Mel Tillis—stuttered all his life.
- American singer, pianist, arranger and songwriter, Ray Charles—contracted glaucoma at an early age and was blind within a year.
- African-American actor, singer and dancer, Sammy Davis, Jr.—lost his left eye in an auto accident in 1954.
- African-American singer and songwriter, Stevie Wonder—was born blind, but he never saw himself at a disadvantage.
- NY Yankee pitcher, Jim Abbott—was born with only one hand. He pitched a no-hitter on September 4, 1993.

These are just a few inspirational figures who pushed beyond their obvious limitations by ignoring them. If these individuals did not allow their handicaps to stop them, why should you?

Maintaining Mental Toughness in Tough Times

How do you handle life's small challenges? Do you attack them halfheartedly? If so, you may underestimate their ability to disrupt your progress in life. Failure to respect the opposition is usually the first harbinger of one's defeat. Mental toughness and cockiness are mutually exclusive mindsets. Mental toughness allows one to size-up opposition—with all its strengths and weaknesses—without crumbling under the assessment. On the other hand, cockiness causes one to rush headlong into the fray without conducting a proper assessment of the matchup.

> A cocky attitude will highlight all of your strengths and show you none of your vulnerabilities.

While I consider courage and belief in one's abilities to be desirable qualities, I feel that we must avoid cockiness at all cost. Cockiness tends always to foreshadow defeat. A cocky attitude will highlight all of your strengths and show you none of your vulnerabilities. It will reveal all of your opponent's weaknesses and blind you to his strengths. It is a deadly trait to possess, for it will never allow you to weigh the heart of an opponent. In battle, courageous hearts often triumph over skill and talent.

To draw an analogy between sports and real life, we must approach the game of life with the same intense execution as professional athletes approach their pursuits on the gridiron or court. If you are to be successful in life, you must demand of yourself no less, in terms of focus on victory. Therefore, begin each day with a sense of urgency so that you keep your eyes on that day's prize.

We are living in tough economic times that are stressing every aspect of our existence. Even the most resilient among us feel the weight of our current woes. To weather the storm of these troubled times, you are going to need mental toughness to maintain a focus on your daily priorities. Today's challenges demand more of our time, money and energy than at any other time in history. Falling behind the proverbial 'eight ball' and then trying to play catch-up often proves to be an exercise in futility.

> Things are rarely as bad as they seem, if you can see every problem as fixable or disposable.

Life's challenges will not cease to bombard you. Therefore, you must endeavor to live each day with a sense of purpose, so that the undercurrents of daily struggle do not sweep you downstream. Trying to maintain one's sanity in today's tough times is a battle all its own. On every conceivable front—family, marriage, financial, workplace, business, education, etc.—people are struggling just to stay afloat.

Just when you think that everything is going fine, some unfortunate incident blindsides you. How do you maintain your focus when your expectations are constantly frustrated and your efforts are seemingly insufficient for the challenge ahead?

Maintaining Mental Toughness in Tough Times

Do not lose your cool! Composure means everything in the midst of chaos. A cooler head will prevail, but a confused mind will further exacerbate the problem. I recently had surgery to repair a hernia. While I was recuperating, a water line broke during the night and flooded two thirds of the first floor of my home. My wife was the first to wake up, only to put her feet into a puddle of water when she began to move about the house.

When I heard my wife's urgent call, my adrenaline immediately began flowing so heavily that I jumped up without the slightest thought of the metal staples in my body or the pain I had been experiencing throughout the night. I quickly discovered the cause of the flood and shut off the water valve, stopping any further damage from occurring. During the entire time I was reacting to this emergency, my mind was in survival mode, keeping me from noticing the pain of my injuries. As soon as I rectified the problem and my adrenaline levels returned to normal, however, I began to feel excruciating pain.

I then called for personal and professional help, as well as my insurance company. Later, I took a couple of pain pills and got some rest. I was disappointed, to say the least, because of the damage. However, I never fell apart or became unraveled throughout the entire ordeal.

For me, life continues to be a precious joy to experience, despite its many challenges. Because I choose to live life according to certain time-tested principles, I am able to maintain a mental toughness that allows me to go through the storms of life without succumbing to them. I will be the first to admit that it is not always easy to face life's struggles and keep a positive mindset. For me, though, the other mental framework is not a pleasant alternative.

Things are rarely as bad as they seem, if you can see every problem as fixable or disposable. Learn to distinguish the difference between what needs repairing and what needs discarding. Developing mental toughness will allow you to react appropriately in either situation.

The Number One Excuse Is....

WHAT DO YOU SUPPOSE IS the number one excuse individuals make for failing to live out their dreams? Do you think the reason is procrastination, lack of resources, want of knowledge, or fear? Without a doubt, every one of these excuses can compete for the top spot, but only one of them can claim the number one spot of all time.

You are correct if you chose fear as the number one excuse people make for not becoming all they are destined to be. Although it is the top excuse used to justify delayed and failed attempts at success, fear is never a legitimate reason. Fear is a paralyzing monster that seeks to drain an individual of self-confidence and self-respect. Fear performs its insidious work on the psyche of a person over an extended period. Without some intervening pattern of thought coming to the rescue, fear will prevent you from moving forward.

> Fear is a paralyzing monster that seeks to drain an individual of self-confidence and self-respect.

Unexpected Treasures

Stephen Graham said, "Excuses are tools of incompetents that build monuments to nothing, and those that specialize in them are seldom good at anything else."

As a young kid, I used to climb trees, scale bridges, and jump down from them without the slightest fear of their height. As I grew older, however, I turned my attention to playing sports, rather than gravity-defying feats. Trying to imitate Spider Man quickly became a faded memory. I can recall helping a couple repair their roof when I was around twenty years old, and I vividly remember being suddenly struck with a paralyzing fear of heights, which had somehow set in at some point between my childhood and that moment. How could this have happened, and where did the fear come from?

I literally became fearful of coming down from the roof of their house. They continued to reassure me that I was only a few feet from the ground, but all I could think of was the view I had while standing on the roof. You see, I am six feet tall—okay, 5'11¾" tall. Nonetheless, standing on the roof gave me the illusion that I was much higher than a mere twelve feet off the ground. In actuality, my feet were only about six feet from the ground, hanging from the gutter. Unfortunately, fear had immobilized me to the point where it took my friends about twenty minutes to talk me down—even while they held my legs for support. At that moment, I became acutely aware of a nemesis within me that would further restrict my possibilities in life, if I did not take decisive action.

Once you recognize fear in your life, you must tackle that demon… much like an aggressive linebacker pursues a defenseless quarterback. Take it out quickly and completely once you detect it. You may not like what you have to do to loosen fear's crippling grip, but you will certainly enjoy the liberty you experience once you do. You will then gain the freedom and confidence to pursue your dreams and tackle your goals in life.

The Rhythm of Life

HAVE YOU EVER LISTENED to a live band and found yourself patting your feet in synch with the beat, only to have some discordant note snatch you from the mood of that moment? Despite their attempts to play through the mistake, your mind detected a break in the intended rhythm of the music. The band quickly becomes unbearable if it continues to hit sour notes and play out of key. Enduring such a performance would require great auditory sacrifice, unless, of course, the unskilled musician happened to be your child at his or her first recital.

Life has a certain rhythm that is easily disrupted when our priorities are out of sync with the destiny we are supposed to pursue. People tend to discover this fact late in the game. When the pursuit of things—money, a career, a person, etc.—fail to bring us the fulfillment we had hoped for, we then realize that things alone can never bring us happiness. Many people falsely assume that happiness is

> Life has a certain rhythm that is easily disrupted when our priorities are out of sync.

the ultimate reward of success. The ultimate reward for your drive and hard work to reach the top depends solely on the priorities you alone set for your life.

In general, people think that their priorities will automatically line up with their dreams, but nothing could be further from the truth. Your priorities will fall in synch with your aspirations when you deliberately place your desires and needs in harmony with your purpose for being on Earth. Once you achieve this delicate balance, you will experience contentment and fulfillment. Therefore, you must order your priorities in a manner that supports your journey in life.

You may be asking, "What is the correct order?" Your life has its own rhythm that suggests how you are to pattern your priorities. It is your responsibility to discover your life's mission, and then you must ensure that you focus primarily on doing those things that best support your purpose. The key is to keep your priorities in perspective.

Two men peered through their prison bars. One man saw only the mud that blanketed the prison yard; the other man saw the many stars that illuminated the night sky! It is often just a matter of perspective. Before you consider changing jobs, churches, or spouses in hopes of finding the fulfillment you seek, examine your attitude. If your attitude is not right, then none of the above will ever matter because *you* will always be the problem.

Each of us has within our being a precious quality that defines and validates our success. God is that Quality; He alone imparts to each of us our own unique rhythm to which we can pat our feet. Start your day with God, and you will never end up out of rhythm or sound off with discordant melody.

Valuable Lessons for Success

ONE OF THE MOST VALUABLE LESSONS you will ever learn is to remain teachable. Learning is essential for the release of your potential, and what you learn is critical for proper growth and balance. One of the main reasons for the large numbers of failed marriages, unsuccessful businesses, declared bankruptcies, and ruined personal lives is the lack of mentorship. The failure to cultivate a relationship with a seasoned individual—preferably a father figure or mentor who is full of wisdom—is often the difference between succeeding or failing in life.

Please, do not misconstrue the point I wish to make here. In no way do I wish to downplay the significant contribution that mothers make in the development of their children. I simply want to point out the value of a father or mentor

> When you have learned how to listen without being quick to judge or interrupt the conversation in midstream, it is a sure sign that you have embraced the first principle of learning.

Unexpected Treasures

(men-tutor). The wisdom of a qualified mentor is priceless. When you have learned how to listen without being quick to judge or interrupt the conversation in midstream, it is a sure sign that you have embraced the first principle of learning, which is… It is better to sit and listen to the greater one than be a person of many words.

The second valuable principle of learning is *follow-through*—following to the letter recommended courses of action, without making assumptions. After hearing the advice from a qualified source, most people tend to over-process the information or attempt to interpret the meaning of the instructions as though the person spoke in a cryptic code. This type of objectionable behavior leads to confusion, frustration, and anger.

I have had only three mentors thus far in my life. I have allowed these individuals to mold my character and to instill in me a sense of purpose. The wisdom and instruction they poured out remain with me to this day, although two of them have gone on to be with the Lord. Each of my mentors came at critical junctures in my life when further growth was necessary. I would certainly not be the man I am today if they had not entered my life when they did. My potential would certainly have withered on the vine and returned unnoticed to the earth.

However, God always has a plan for our lives, and His plans always come to us in sentence fragments and broken paragraphs. I know you may want to ask, "What do you mean by fragments and broken paragraphs?" Simply this—the fragments oftentimes reveal only very small parts of the puzzle for your future. The broken paragraphs are then the words given to provide more clarity and instruction; they advise you on what to do from where you are, and how to prepare only for the next stage of your life. God will never reveal His plan for you in motion pictures; you can only view it one frame at a time.

Mentorship helps to shorten your learning process. What may have taken your mentor twenty years to learn, you may find yourself mastering the same skill or trade in just a few short years, or less—but only if you embrace your mentor's instructions.

Learn to listen. Embrace a God-sent mentor!

My Protégé's Mistake

ONE DAY ONE OF MY PROTÉGÉS approached me for my advice regarding a pressing problem he had been having. Because of his desperate plea for direction, I decided to give him my full attention. He revealed that if he did not make an immediate decision about the matter, it could cost him a considerable amount of money. Upon hearing the entire issue, I recommended that he call the company first thing in the morning to present his case to them and then propose a remedial solution. Furthermore, I suggested that he follow-up the telephone conversation with a detailed email message, recapping what he had discussed on the phone. After several days had passed, I saw the individual and inquired about what actions he had taken concerning his problem.

> If you pursue nothing in life, life will produce NOTHING to enjoy.

He said that he and his wife decided to hold off on making any decision and that they would call the company next week. I asked, "Do you think that your problem is going to go away?" He replied, "These things have a funny way of working themselves out." I responded with utter silence and concluded the conversation with, "Good Day."

How can people be so naïve as to think that problems will improve without diligent attention? Has any problem ever evolved into something better without the care of a concerned mind? That notion makes as much sense as The Big Bang Theory, which postulates that the ordered beauty we see in nature is the result of a random bang that occurred in the cosmos. The last time I checked, violent explosions leave only chaos and ruin in their wake.

Are you the kind of person who leaves his problems alone, hoping they will improve on their own? The person who lives this way is counting on luck to solve all his or her problems. Some people do seem to enjoy some unfair advantages when it comes to succeeding in life. However, the truth is that success yields its bounty to those who are self-disciplined, driven by passion, and who believe they are entitled to enjoy all that life has to offer.

E. B. White said, "Luck is not something you can mention in the presence of self-made men."

In the book of Joshua, God informed Joshua that he would know good success and make his way prosperous if he would simply adhere to God's laws and only be courageous. No marriage works without sacrifice; no business succeeds without a proven product or service; and no person overcomes ignorance without replacing it with information and applied knowledge. Therefore, get your head out of the sand and make something happen.

Lucille Ball once said, "Luck? I don't know anything about luck. I've never banked on it, and I'm afraid of people who do. Luck to me is something else: Hard work—and realizing what is opportunity and what isn't."

It is easy to blame others for your lack of success because it absolves you of any responsibility for your fate in life. If you pursue nothing in life, NOTHING will be what you enjoy.

Develop Your
Full Potential

DO YOU EVER ASK YOURSELF why you find it difficult to reach your full potential? I am certain that you can recall certain people—a teacher, a coach, a mentor, or even a friend—in your life who would constantly point out the great potential you possessed. Oftentimes, others are quick to identify what we fail recognize about ourselves. In all honesty, most people are too afraid to explore their God-given potential, for fear of where it may lead them.

> Potential is hidden deep within the crevices of a person's natural ability–which some call talent.

Potential vs. Talent

Potential is not something that we have readily at our disposal; it does not stand idly by for our use whenever we need it. It exists only as mere possibility, which we must pull to the surface of our being and then nurture to the point where we can then call it…ability. Potential is hidden deep within the crevices of a person's natural ability—which some call talent.

God-given talent is the natural ability to do a thing effortlessly, seemingly without much thought. However, potential is unrealized ability that we usually never harvest. Potential is that marginal difference that separates truly great talent from simply good ability. Where potential exists, ability is also present to perform, albeit on a much lower rung. Extracting the hidden potential from talent takes a great deal of effort, which is why so few people become great at anything.

Wanting More...

"I feel as though I can do anything and become anyone I want to be. I see other people far less talented succeeding and enjoying the kind of life I wish to enjoy. It is not that I am lazy, but some unseen force keeps holding me back from going full speed ahead. It's become so frustrating, wanting more out of life but never fully going for it."

Does this sound like you? Incompetence and low self-esteem are not the reason for your lack of success. It may very well be that you are among the more talented people with great potential to succeed. However, your challenge is that while you may have a passion pushing you in one direction to achieve a certain goal, you also have other competing interests pulling you in the opposite direction. The net effect is that you achieve nothing. Trying to chase two rabbits at the same time will ensure that you catch neither of them—expending tremendous energy, with little to show for it.

Less Talented, but More Successful

A lack of focus will cause you to dabble with irrelevant activities that serve only to siphon off productivity from the things you should pursue. In the end, you always have very little to show for your efforts. Although there are many people with far less talent than you, they succeed because they are able to maintain focus on one goal until they reach it. Accomplishment of any magnitude is difficult to achieve without consistent follow-through.

Develop Your Full Potential

Potential Scattered

Your failure to reach your full potential may not be the result of a lack of passion. It may very well be that your energies and focus are now scattered because of all of the extraneous projects you take on. Additionally, you may be prone to fixating only on one thing too long, not able to multi-task. Therefore, whenever you devote your attention to multiple tasks, not only do you divide your focus, but you also dilute your productivity and effectiveness. The result is that many things go undone.

Potential is useless if individuals never recognize they have it.

> Potential is useless if individuals never recognize they have it.

Fix It

To remedy your problem, you need only to maintain the focus that will keep your passion behind your efforts. When other ideas and interests come your way, simply prioritize them with respect to your main objectives in life. If they serve to get you closer to your goals, keep them high on your list of priorities. However, if they, cause you to veer away from your intended course, then place them near the bottom or remove them from your list altogether.

Because our minds crave variety, you must force yourself to focus on the mission at hand. Fight to remain mentally focused on your main objectives, and you will begin to see your potential turn into the talent that will make your dreams come true.

Avoiding Seven
Destructive Financial Patterns

How can people complain about being deeply in debt when they needlessly spend money on luxury items that they could not afford in the first place, such as gigantic flat screen televisions? What makes this kind of purchase equally as bad is that they purchase this item on credit. On the other hand, consider the person who wantonly purchases items without giving thought to whether his or her bank account can cover the expenditures. In either case, impulsivity controls the spending behavior.

I appreciate the individual who chooses to place honoring his debt obligations before self-indulgent spending, especially when the debt has to do with honoring a pledge or vow made to the church, a relative, or a friend. I believe strongly that paying your commercial creditors is just as important as paying a debt to the church or to another person. However, the majority

> Gaining control over impulsive spending is the only cure for the person who derives pleasure from such destructive behavior.

of financial difficulties that families encounter stem from individuals living beyond their means, as a result of giving in to the temptation of seductive merchant marketing and advertising campaigns. Therefore, honor the debt you have vowed to pay to God, to your fellow man, and to commercial lending institutions—in that order—to the degree that you can without suffering any undue legal difficulties.

In many instances, married couples experience financial problems because one of the spouses believes that payday means spending day. As long as the bank account has money in it, he or she is entitled to purchase whatever that individual chooses. Payday should not serve as the stimulus that sets spending in motion. Rather, it should be an occasion to satisfy necessary monthly bill obligations as well as an opportunity to begin to accumulate wealth.

Many shopaholics live in a state of constant denial regarding their condition. They will blame everyone and everything else for their predicament, without realizing *they* are the problem. Their compulsion to spend money will eventually destroy everything around them, including valued personal relationships. Gaining control over impulsive spending is the only cure for the person who derives pleasure from such destructive behavior. This problem is more pervasive in our society than you can imagine.

Here are seven indicators to help you assess whether you have fallen victim to certain financially destructive behavior:

1. You become unusually happy when you have money.
2. You start spending money before you get your hands on it.
3. You become defensive whenever money is the focus of discussion.
4. You look at family income as your income.
5. You seldom ask about the family bills.
6. You always suspect that your spouse is hiding money from you.
7. You are very judgmental with regard to how others manage their money.

Avoiding Seven Financial Destructive Patterns

These are just seven signposts to indicate where you stand, though there are many others. While the impulsive spender or the shopaholic may periodically exhibit signs of rationality when it comes to handling money, they will eventually repeat their destructive ways—if there is no intervention is sought.

Now What?

What if you could erase all of your bad habits...would you? Unfortunately, our bad habits only disappear when we replace them with healthy ones; and that part takes some effort...sorry to say.

Invariably, you will experience slight discomfort as you act to rid yourself of destructive behavior that is doing nothing but ruining your life and robbing you of bright tomorrows. Most people are not even aware of the destructive behavior they live with on a daily basis. Furthermore, they have little knowledge of the damage their bad habits are inflicting on everyone and everything around them. Rarely do their actions only affect themselves.

If you believe that you live with a destructive habit, do not be afraid to reach out for help. In doing so, you will discover that your courageous actions will help more than just yourself; it may serve to reclaim a troubled marriage or friendship. Who knows...just take action now!

Does Your Paycheck Reflect Your Self-Esteem?

IT IS DANGEROUS TO HAVE SOMETHING and not know what you have. It is even more treacherous to know what you have and then do nothing with it. We often bury priceless dreams and talents beneath counter-productive, low self-esteem. People who struggle with low self-esteem also tend to earn low incomes. Additionally, low self-esteem contributes significantly to a person's lack of motivation and desire to escape from the pattern of negative thinking that perpetuates mediocrity.

Although most people will suffer from the effects of having a low self-esteem all their lives, hope does exist for those brave individuals who take decisive action to increase the worth they attach to themselves. If you suffer from feelings of low self-worth, act

> If you suffer from feelings of low self-worth, act now to change your self-perception because too much is riding on how you see yourself.

now to change your self-perception because too much is riding on how you see yourself.

The Advantage of Change

With patience and a little effort, you can raise your self-esteem to a healthy level. A healthy self-image gives you the confidence to pursue opportunities aggressively. When a person ceases to focus all his attention on his internal state, possibilities seem to appear from nowhere. Your horizons become much broader and clearer, as you free yourself to delve deeper into the limitless depths of your potential.

Self-esteem is an underrated and undervalued commodity. Your production and resulting income will always be much lower than it should be whenever you undervalue your own worth. As a result, you will to tend to shortchange yourself in your financial dealings. Coming up short in any economy will lead to frustrations in other areas of life.

Your Actions Reflect Your Thoughts

Average people give average effort. Let me also say it this way…certain people will only ever enjoy an average life because average is all they choose to exchange for labor's reward. You cannot expect extraordinary results by giving ordinary effort. What you think of yourself determines how hard you push to achieve your goals; but it will also dictate how high you are willing to aim. It is impossible to have high expectations while wrestling with a low self-esteem. The law of reflection is as real as the law of gravity. Your life mirrors what you think and believe. You will never possess more in life than you truly believe you deserve. Remember…

> "If you can control a man's thinking, you don't have to worry about his actions. If you can determine what a man thinks, you do not have worry about what he will do. If you can make a man believe that he is inferior, you don't have to compel him to seek an inferior status, he will do so without being told; and if you can make a man believe

Does Your Paycheck Reflect Your Self Esteem?

that he is justly an outcast, you don't have to order him to the back door, he will go to the back door on his own; and if there is no back door, the very nature of the man will demand that you build one."

—Carter G. Woodson

You Can Do It! It's Not Too Late

WHEN YOUR AGE BECOMES more than a number and it stops you from pursuing your dreams, simply consider the inspiring story of one of my mentees, Mrs. G. Proctor, who happens to be a septuagenarian.

While in her 70s, she lost her husband of many years. His funeral alone left behind more bills than she had money to cover. She worked part time for a national company, selling household accessories, but the job provided only a small supplemental income. While she was not struggling financially, she felt the crunch coming on. However, as she started attending my Dream Makers 99 (DM99) conclaves frequently, she began to feel a stirring on the inside in response to many of the things I would share. At first, she questioned whether age would prevent her from owning a business.

> It is better to start one thing and finish it than never to start and finish anything.

Unexpected Treasures

At a particular DM99 conclave, I shared how some people start businesses later in life because they are late bloomers. I recall saying, "It is better to start one thing and finish it than never to start and finish anything," trying to allay the concerns that many older people have about pursuing their dreams. I mentioned how Colonel Sanders started the famous Kentucky Fried Chicken fast food chain when he was sixty-five years of age. I commented that any age is the right age to begin a business as long as you have the stamina and desire to see your vision through to fruition. That day, precious Mrs. Proctor took my advice and began in earnest to act.

Shortly after that particular DM99 conclave, she met a woman who owned a *Curves* fitness center. Wanting to leave the business, the owner asked my mentee if she would be interested in purchasing the facility. Mrs. Proctor immediately sought my advice. Because she was unable to answer many of my initial questions, I told her to go back and research the business. Satisfied that she had done her due diligence, I offered my advice concerning her investment options. When she told me the woman's initial asking price, I simply said, "No! It is too high." I then recommended that she present a ridiculously low counteroffer to the owner. Mrs. Proctor knew that the other woman would accept nothing less than $30K—this being half of her original asking price.

There was only one problem. She did not have $30K. Instead, she had faith in God, me as her business coach, and the guts to believe she could own her own business. Desperate, she felt that if she did not take this woman's offer immediately, she would lose the deal. I simply said, "If you cannot walk away from this, then the owner has you and your money." I told her to go back to the woman to express her interest, but feign strong concern about the fact that her fitness center was actually losing money and that assuming it would be a risky proposition. I told her to stand firm in her offer, regardless of how ridiculous it appeared. Mrs. Proctor thought I was out of my mind. She quipped, "That woman would never accept such a low offer." I simply said, "How do you know?

You Can Do It! It's Not Too Late

Are you a mind reader?" Later she told me how she walked away thinking I was out of my mind. Nevertheless, she carried out my instructions, and today she is the proud owner of her own *Curves* franchise, and she paid less than $20K for it.

It is never too late to begin living your dreams.

A Simple Twist to Upgrade Your Money Potential

IT IS EXTREMELY DIFFICULT to remain motivated to work for a paycheck you have already spent, especially when the money is going towards something you do not even need. Money may not bring you happiness, but it certainly enables you to look for it in plenty of places. Moreover, the feeling we get from the things money provides bears a close resemblance to happiness. Do not misunderstand me! I do not love money; I simply like it a lot. People who claim not to like money will often lie about many other things, as well. I merely like the time-saving conveniences and numerous opportunities that money affords me.

> People who claim not to like money will often lie about many other things as well.

Managing Your Money

You may be wondering why the subject of money is so important to me. The truth is…I realize that I have an important mandate on my life to help as many people succeed financially as I can before I depart this Earth. Part of my purpose in life is to impart my wisdom on financial increase into the lives of those who will receive it. I truly am more interested in your success than your adoration.

Managing and keeping money requires more skill than earning it. It behooves each and every one of us to become a good money manager because you have the highest vested interest in how well your money performs in the marketplace. The wealthy have many concerns, but theirs look very different than those of the poor and middle-class. With the poor, obtaining money is a hounding thought; with the middle class, getting it to stretch is a consuming notion; but with the wealthy, getting it to travel farther is an exciting occupation of energy and thought. Wealthy individuals play the money game to win while others simply play not to lose.

Poor, Middle Class, and Wealthy Mind Sets

People with a poor perspective on money matters tend to always be in survival mode when it comes to living life. Their primary goal is to have enough money to pay their bills on time and stash away ample funds to afford a vacation. On the other hand, a healthy approach to money management causes individuals to amass wealth, not just an income. These individuals are committed to wealth accumulation—not debt accumulation. While poor and middle-class people may want to enjoy financial prosperity, it is the wealthy individuals who consistently demonstrate their commitment to producing it. If you are not totally committed to creating wealth, chances are you will not. Most Americans know exactly how it feels when their money is funny, but there is nothing funny when your money does not meet your basic needs.

> There is nothing funny when your money does not meet your basic needs.

Changing Tracks

If you want to change your money condition, you have to change what you are doing, keeping in mind that the information you rely upon will always channel you in a certain direction in life. Your thoughts are the railroad tracks upon which your life travels. You travel from one station to another in life based on the kind of thoughts running through your mind. Your life can only move in the direction of the tracks of your thoughts. No train can travel far without tracks; neither can you. Your thoughts will take you wherever you want to go.

Give me five minutes with any person and I can tell you if they are going far in life. When people are not satisfied with their financial condition, they will do one of two things. They will either complain incessantly about their situation, or they will shut up and do something about it.

Altering Your Mentality

Become passionate about changing your mentality about money. A healthy regard for money is the first step toward understanding it. Wanting more money does not signify greed; it merely underscores our inherent yearning for progression and expansion that God gave to us at birth. Without this natural drive to produce more, we would not pursue the creative thoughts in our minds and we would all be stuck living in caves or traveling great distances by way of our two feet.

Our basic human nature causes our eyes to crave what they see, our hands to stretch for what lies beyond reach, our ears to bend in the direction of sound, our tongues to salivate at the idea of a hearty repast, and our minds to travel far and wide to explore new horizons. Similarly, a healthy outlook on money will cause you to journey in the direction of the wealth that is possible for you to enjoy.

Killing Two Birds with One Stone

A woman I know—who at one time could never keep her checkbook straight—has solved her problem very neatly. Her method is rather unorthodox, but it is one that has enabled her to set up a Christmas shopping fund, as well. All she does is balance her checkbook without recording the cents. For example, if a bill is for $7.20, she writes a check for that amount. However, she records $8 in the checkbook ledger, instead of $7.20. If the amount is for $10.34, she enters $11 to be subtracted from the prior balance. In effect, she is rounding every check up to the next dollar amount. What seems insignificant produces great results over time.

At the end of the first month, after writing numerous personal checks, she accumulated roughly $20 in this way. By the end of the year, she was able to take those hidden profits and turn them into a nice little Christmas fund. By the way…her checkbook never again came up short.

Turbocharge Your Life

WHAT IS THE SOURCE OF YOUR strength and influence? What do you do to revive your zest for life? Everyone is energized by something in life. Some draw strength and excitement from cheering on a favorite team while others may get it simply by watching a movie, like Rocky. Whatever the case, you must find your source of motivation.

Athletes at all levels use music and certain meditation techniques to prepare mentally for competition. Theatre and screen actors find their motivation in getting to know intimately the characters they portray. Singers reveal that they get over nervousness by focusing on an object in the concert hall until they lose those pre-show jitters. We are aware of what these people do to crystallize focus or summon passion, but what do *you* do to get your gears in motion.

> Most people live defeated lives because they ignore the tools that are meant to empower them.

Unexpected Treasures

Are you ready for me to reveal to you the secrets that will ignite a passion within you to improve your life and everything in it? I knew your response would be, "YES!" Most people live defeated lives because they ignore the tools that are meant to empower them. If the biblical character, King David, knew how to encourage and motivate himself in the Lord, you had better wake up to the reality of self-motivation. When no one is there to celebrate your life, you need to know how to celebrate yourself, unapologetically.

Every seed bears the potential to produce a fully mature harvest of whatever the seed is. Contrary to common belief, fish do not learn to swim in a school of fish. Birds may flock together, but their flocking does not teach any of them to fly. Fish swim and birds fly because of innate abilities that God placed within them. Similarly, you have innate abilities that you may not even be aware of. For example, the ability to encourage yourself in tough times is part of your makeup. The integrity of your character resides within your creation. True character is what holds up talent under the weight of public scrutiny.

Talent is simply a capacity filled with potential. Most people display a great deal of raw talent, but they never tap into the hidden potential that is waiting to kick-in to sustain them through adversity. Oftentimes, we call upon talent to do what only unrefined potential exists to do, and when we look to our talent to bail us out of tight jams, it often fails us. In order to overcome the challenges that life will throw your way, you must take a different approach to winning in life. If your old tools and methods for overcoming obstacles constantly leave you defeated and unable to keep pace with today's challenges, you are in need of a turbocharger in your daily routine.

Do you know why 10 percent of the people own 90 percent of the economic pie in America? The reason is that the ten percent exercise the willingness to change, adapt and maintain an attitude conducive to winning. Most people do not like change. Resistance to change is the natural inclination of most people, regardless of the benefits that certain change brings. General Motors refused to shift gears by responding to the public's demand for smaller vehicles. As a result, GM has since paid a heavy price in showrooms all across this country. In the early eighties, IBM refused to notice a growing trend for personal computers, and the giant company soon found itself overrun by more agile and consumer-sensitive competition.

When you are married to methods, change will never be accepted. In today's tight economy, one cannot afford to overlook the signs that portend change in consumer appetite. Do not allow yourself to become entrenched in old methods if they no longer address today's needs. Today's savvy consumers are not as forgiving as they once were. If you do not adjust to changing times, your outdated products or services will pile up on the shelves.

Do not become stubborn, and avoid rejecting new concepts and approaches to doing old things in new ways. Holding fast to outmoded technologies and practices can doom you to the junkyard if you lose touch with everything around you. Reluctance to change may in fact mask a heart filled with an arrogance that says I am too good or proficient at what I do to ever be overrun by innovation. I can assure you that no amount of experience will spare you from getting the pink slip if you choose not to remain relevant.

> Do not allow yourself to become entrenched in old methods if they no longer address today's needs.

Listen to me carefully…you cannot fake winning or succeeding in life. When your life is in the dumps, believe me, your life is in the dumps. But I want to leave you with seven things I do to turbocharge my life every single day:

1. I pray every day and ask God to show me the things I should do that would allow me to complete the big picture.
2. I make a constant decision to remain relevant and enthusiastic about the future.

3. I keep in mind the fact that God will not place more on me than I can bear.
4. I make a concerted effort every day to walk by faith and not by sight.
5. Each day I locate the joy of the Lord, for it is my strength.
6. I speak words filled with purpose, those intended only to teach, exhort, or create.
7. I read fervently to stretch my mind, so that I can envision the future I want to live.

Doing these seven things habitually emboldens me to attack life aggressively. Additionally, they provide me with balance in a sea of uncertainty, calm in the midst of my storms, and discipline to refrain from giving in to temptation. Practice them and you too will experience victory on a daily basis.

The Quiet Character of a Strong Woman

I HAVE LIVED MUCH OF MY LIFE around some rather strong and remarkable women who have achieved remarkable success under some of the most difficult circumstances. Women, in general, have an amazing capacity to endure great adversity while doing whatever they must do in order to accomplish their goals in life. When you factor children in the equation, women have historically demonstrated an unmatched ability to ascend to death-defying heights of self-sacrifice to defend and provide for their families.

First Self-made Female Millionaire

Madam C. J. Walker, a very successful entrepreneur, philanthropist, and social activist around the turn of the twentieth century, was a person whose life was a profile of courage and intestinal

> Men learn many valuable lessons from their dads, but in most cases, they draw strength from their mothers.

fortitude. She succeeded against the odds in business at a time in America when blacks were treated as second-class citizens. In 1904, after hearing the famed Booker T. Washington speak, Sarah Breedlove (Madam Walker's name at the time) was inspired to go into business for herself. A few months later, Sarah perfected the recipe for a hair care product that could straighten black women's hair. Shortly thereafter, she began conducting hair-straightening demonstrations with a steel hot comb given to her by one of her clothes-washing clients, and her business soon took off. With a steady stream of satisfied customers who also wanted a portion of her scalp formula for their use at home, Madam Walker began dishing out the concoction to them in tin cups.

It is worth noting that her ability to recognize a need, develop a winning product, and sell it to the masses was the key to her becoming the first female in history (not simply the first black woman) to earn millionaire status based on her own achievements, as cited by *The Guinness Book of Records*.

Near the end of her life on July, 1912 at a National Negro Business League Convention, she reflected on her amazing accomplishments by saying:

> "I am a woman who came from the cotton fields of the South. From there I was promoted to the washtub. From there I was promoted to the cook kitchen. And from there I promoted myself into the business of manufacturing hair goods and preparations…I have built my own factory on my own ground."

A Great Private School

My lovely wife, Debra, is an amazing, strong, and very intelligent woman who is presently living her dream—besides being married to me—of running her own preschool and academy. As a young student, she worked her way through Hampton University, graduating with a nursing degree. Afterward, she served six years as an Army nurse, attaining the rank of Captain. Upon exiting the military, she entered the private sector and began quickly to climb the corporate ladder as a healthcare administrator. Resisting the lure of a six-figure promotion, she decided instead to follow her heart and open a private academy (preschool thru high school) to provide children with a solid Christian-based education, with nothing but a dream and her faith in God.

And despite my many pleas for her to delay the process of starting the school for six months, she remained adamant in her position to begin immediately, saying, "If not now, then when." Determined not to be sidetracked, she plowed full steam ahead, establishing one of our city's top-ranked private schools.

The Most Influential Woman in the World

I cannot go any further without bringing into focus one of the most successful women of our time, Oprah Winfrey. She overcame the shame and indignity of being raped and molested very early in her life to rise to prominence in the male-dominated industry of talk show television, relying on nothing but her keen business instincts and her gifted speaking abilities. She has since been able to cross racial and gender barriers to become one of the top ten most influential persons in America.

Mothers Influence

Down through the centuries, mothers have influenced the lives of their children far more than fathers have. I am not saying that fathers have not had an impact on their children, but mothers are far more nurturing than fathers are. When athletes are being interviewed, they will usually say, "Hi Mom!" to the camera. Women have endured physical and verbal abuse, rape, low wages, and sundry other forms of humiliation, and yet they rise from all this degradation. Most women know very well how to get up after being knocked down by hurt and disappointment—this being their usual experience.

My Mother's Endurance

I learned very early in life what true strength of character was all about by watching my mother fight through adversity and disappointment on many occasions. I never once saw her give up during times of dire poverty or periods of prolonged unemployment. While working at Western Electric and raising four rambunctious boys, she always sought better job opportunities. She never used not having a high school diploma as an excuse not to provide for her children. She would eventually find stable work at the US Post Office and work there long enough to retire.

A Life Lesson from my Mother

My mother instilled in us essential qualities that are noticeably absent in many people today. Once, she threatened to wear out my behind if I did not return to school the next day and face a kid who had beaten me up the day before. Her threat filled me with a determination to never again allow anyone to beat me up the way that boy had. I have since learned that when life pushes you, you must push back even harder. With a tough mom like mine, how could I have developed any other way?

A Woman's Value

Men learn many valuable lessons from their dads, but in most cases, they draw strength from their mothers. This generation has experienced a drastic decline in the number of strong women in our society. There are many sociological factors that account for this phenomenon. Young girls today need to connect with strong women mentors because most of their role models on television are nothing more than glitzy façades. Neither your money nor your career can determine your worth. A woman's worth is in her birth. Her character alone reveals the internal standards and strength she has at her disposal in times of adversity.

A woman who refuses to compare herself to others will never make the mistake of competing with them. She knows who she is, and she is comfortable in her own skin. She may have made mistakes early in life, and no doubt she will continue to make many more, but she somehow continues to get up and find the strength to push the reset button on life.

And somehow, by the grace of God, her tenacity allows her to witness her mistakes turn into miracles.

Making This Year Your Best Year Yet!

When it comes to improving your life, you cannot afford to approach the matter nonchalantly. If your life is in need of radical transformation, then you must employ drastic measures to produce the needed change. Desperate times call for desperate measures. If what you attempted last year left you with nothing more than a need for more New Year's resolutions, then scrap those vain efforts that are never fulfilled. However, if you sincerely desire to reduce your weight, make more money, or improve your marital relationship, you must fuel those desires with a kick-butt, take-no-prisoners attitude.

> Living the ultimate life is not synonymous with living a life of defeat.

Live the Ultimate Life

Divorce yourself from self-defeating and counterproductive behavior, so that you can begin to live the ultimate life you dream of. I must warn you, though, that when you decide to eliminate the obstacles that continue to thwart your progress, you will begin to stand out from those who wish to continue to live in mediocrity. Living the ultimate life is not synonymous with living a life of defeat. Instead, it equates to living life to your full potential and enjoying the scenery along the way—the landscape that mirrors what is in your heart.

Destroy Toxic Thinking

It is the toxic thinking that comes from being in the wrong atmosphere that causes people to believe that it is okay to fall short of their goals and aspirations. In actuality, it is never alright to miss the mark of achieving your dreams in life. Why set goals with no intention of ever reaching them. Setting out in life with this attitude is both a waste of time and energy. Adjusting your standards and expectations upward is the necessary precursor to substantive change, and it is the first step you must take if you are to move closer to your dreams. You must envision yourself defying the odds that are stacked against your success, and then you must take comfort in knowing that what you can imagine enjoying is indeed possible for you to begin living.

General MacArthur's Warrior Mentality

American Civil War General William Tecumseh Sherman once declared, "War is hell"—perhaps because wartime rules of engagement are usually scrapped on the battlefield, where life-and-death decisions are made in an instant. The mentality most prevalent in war is kill or be killed. When it comes to battling those enemies that constantly try to kill your passion and dreams, you must take the same survival mentality as the soldier in battle. You must determine that you will not return from war with anything short of victory.

A Couple's Misfortune

I am reminded of a married couple in their early forties who momentarily succumbed to the ravages of this failing economy. After he experienced a significant pay cut and she lost her job to overseas competition, they found themselves struggling to make ends meet and to hold onto their home. Falling seven months behind on their mortgage payments, the couple could no longer avoid the dreaded foreclose process; the lender was forced to take action. At first, they were very disgusted with the entire mortgage lending system, and they concluded that there was no hope until… I encouraged them to turn their anger into productive energy by learning to make the system work in their favor. In the end, they took advantage of my advice, saved their home, and got back on track with their credit. This couple's story had a happy ending because they decided to cease being the victims of misfortune.

How to Subjugate Misfortune

Anger and resentment will oftentimes cloud your perspectives and leave you incapable of recognizing opportunities that exist in the midst of misfortune. Remember, there is always fortune to be gleaned from misfortune. You just have to be diligent in looking for it.

As long as there is still life in you and fight in your spirit, you always have an opportunity to turn around your misfortune. However, it is imperative that you begin to explore the treasure God has hidden inside of you. You can start by focusing on your known strengths. They will often hold the key that can unlock the door to your breakthrough moment. It does not matter when things turn in your favor; it just matters that you move aggressively to set in motion the requisite activity that will get the ball rolling. You will soon begin to attract the desires of your heart as a result of this changed mindset.

> It does not matter when things turn in your favor; it just matters that it does.

Misfortune Defeated

Let us revisit the couple who stared down foreclosure and won. They fought back instead of taking it! They paused long enough in their misfortune to recognize a weakness and discover how to become better money managers. They negotiated with the mortgage company to change its credit reporting of the foreclosure situation. This took some time, but the couple was successful in regaining their creditworthiness. To top things off, they started a home business that is bringing them even closer together. If you look hard enough, you will discover that every cloud does have a silver lining in it. Find it and you can make every bad situation work for you instead of against you.

The Biggest Loser

Whatever you do, never compare your situation to that of others. While our difficulties may have a similar plot, I can assure you that the scripts are never the same. When it comes to losing weight, do not fall into the trap of measuring your efforts against the jaw-dropping results of those contestants on The Biggest Loser reality show. These individuals must commit to six months of grueling 6- to 8-hour-a-day workouts while feasting on foods prepared by expert dietitians.

Remember, your circumstances are quite different. You do not have the luxury, in most cases, of spending that much time in a gym. Neither do you have someone preparing specially designed meals to jump-start your metabolism and accelerate your weight loss. Your daily routine requires that you must discipline yourself and that you maintain a workout plan that will allow you to achieve your fitness goals.

Be encouraged by the fact that you can still lose all the weight you desire, regardless of how many times you may have failed to meet your goals in the past. This time, you must approach your situation with a different mentality. You must tell yourself, "If I can put it on, I can take it off." I hold to the notion that if there is a recipe for disaster, there must be a formula for success. Discover that formula for whatever you aim to do in life so that you can make this your best year yet.

Hopefully you realize that this whole section on weight loss was simply a metaphor for how you should approach every challenge in your life. Simply define your desired end result; develop a practical plan to achieve it; and then just stick to it.

It is that simple.

Understanding the Power of Endurance

A GOOD COACH IS FOREMOST a good teacher who sets tough standards and expects his students to meet them. You do not teach individuals to respect governing standards, laws, rules, and principles by lowering them in order to accommodate substandard performers. Because nearly everything we do in life entails learning or teaching of some sort, it behooves us to enforce the type of standards that will ensure the kind of results we expect to see in society.

Over the years, many men and women have come into my life to teach me important life lessons. They would later reveal that they took time to counsel me because they saw potential they did not want to see me waste. Even today, many teachers share how they identify countless students with great potential but who have very little desire to achieve academically. The problem is that our public schools continue to lower their academic standards to accommodate the students' deficiencies.

> You can decide to become bitter or better when injustice and misfortune come your way.

Consequently, students approach life believing that it will also accommodate their substandard output. When life resists and pushes back very hard, most of them tend to surrender to apathy. Unable to make a difference, they become complacent with mediocrity. What we then have in society are people who avoid at all cost the challenge to explore their intellectual curiosity and reach beyond the limits of their circumstances for change. However, effective mentoring can turn around this disturbing trend.

I mentor and routinely provide guidance to young men who come from very troubled pasts—men who made the tough choice to beat the odds. Growing up fatherless is one of many excuses they often cite to justify their lack of desire to succeed in life. I approach these men by first getting them to understand that continuing to blame their present circumstances on their past conditions only condemns their future to more misery. Once they accept this fact, then and only then can substantive change take place.

Nelson Mandela spent twenty-seven years incarcerated in a South African prison for fighting against an Apartheid system that stripped South African blacks of their basic human rights. Upon his release from prison, it was evident that he remained just as focused and determined to pursue the same cause that had taken his freedom twenty-seven years earlier. When you endure extreme injustices and adversities, you must determine to exit them better, not bitter...as Mandela did.

The dignified Nelson Mandela displayed no signs of hatred or bitterness. What is more remarkable is how he used twenty-seven years of captivity to turn a negative situation into a positive one. His composure under such prolonged adversity was, no doubt, what caused many South Africans to elect him (only four years after his release) as the first president—and first black president—of a democratic South Africa. His achievement is without precedent, but it serves as a constant reminder that perseverance can always outlast persecution.

You can decide to become bitter or better when injustice and misfortune come your way. However, if you will stay the course, you will receive the just recompense of your endurance.

A Good Person Cannot Be Kept Down

NEVER JUDGE A PERSON BASED ON his or her present station in life—believing it to be their permanent condition. Oftentimes, people wrongly conclude that their mistakes have sentenced them to a lifetime of failure. The result is that many unwise bystanders sit on the sidelines, judging and predicting the futures of the ones they have condemned to a life of doom.

For example, negative media reports influenced many people to rush to judgment and conclude prematurely that Kobe Bryant was guilty of sexually assaulting 19-year old Katelyn Faber, who was a hotel employee at the time. At the beginning of the summer of 2003, Kobe found himself embroiled in a sexual assault case that caused many of his high-profile endorsers to jump ship, taking their lucrative contracts with them. Does it ever dawn on those individuals who are quick to judge that the majority of what they hear from others (especially the media) is second, third, or even tenth generation information? The truth is that

> Critics are not worth the time and energy most people give them.

you cannot rely on this kind of information to make a fair and reasonable assessment of a person's character or future, for that matter. I am not condoning Kobe Bryant's indiscretion; I am simply making a case that failure does not necessarily dictate crisis or that one's future is done.

Nineteen years ago, I went through a divorce that devastated me to the core, both personally and financially. To everyone who knew me then, I looked as though I was down for the count, never to recover. However, God had other things in mind for me. Without doubt, God restored me to an even greater level of respect and financial standing in my community. He was and is my recovery plan in the midst of any storm. Not only did I recover ground, I also gained a wonderful wife and a much healthier self-esteem after the ordeal ended.

Many individuals watched my plight from the sidelines, offering play-by-play commentary on all my failures and struggles. The talk abounded regarding what I had done to trigger such devastation. Needless to say, the rumor mill never spit out one shred of information about my situation that was anywhere close to the truth.

Because of what I endured throughout that divorce episode, I concluded that if a man can get up from his failures, he lives to fight another day. Therefore, continue to fight your way through the negative debris and false commentary that seeks to destroy your self-esteem whenever you go through difficult times.

Your critics love nothing more than for you to stay down after life delivers a knock-out punch. On some warped level, they get a kick out of predicting your demise. Give them no such satisfaction. Get up! Critics are not worth the time and energy most people give them. Instead, prove to yourself that you have the wherewithal to rebound from your trials, which are merely common to every man—as the Bible declares.

Whenever you go through difficulty, ask God to help you; believe, and He will. Remember…with God, all things are possible.

May the Force Be with You

17

VISION IS ONE OF THE MOST galvanizing forces you can ever have, for it has the potential to rouse in you the drive and passion to pursue your greatest aspirations. Vision is the reason for perseverance, the basis for pensive thought, and the object of distant dreams. Vision is not a mere wishful thought, but a glimpse into your tomorrows.

Everyone has vision, but not all will cultivate their vision so that it can generate the greatest possibilities imaginable. The vision that most people have reveals not much more than their desire to pay their bills on time while enjoying a comfortable lifestyle. On the other hand, some people envision themselves with the financial means to assist hundreds or even thousands of others in paying their bills—by way of the jobs their dreams create. It all boils down to one's scope on

> A broader scope of your tomorrows will leave a larger footprint on the earth, but it will also require more tenacity to see it manifest.

the future. A broader scope of your tomorrows will leave a larger footprint on the Earth, but it will also require more tenacity to see it manifest.

Leaders must maintain clear perspective and focus at all times to avoid leading their followers aimlessly through the wilderness of life. Vision reveals the destination of your travels, but the goals you set represent the arterial highways along which must you travel to get there.

Vision comes to us in the form of thoughts, but the thoughts have everything to do with places, things, and people in our future. Your vision can reveal a building, a business franchise, a car, a jet plane, a university, a man landing on the moon, etc. When you see vision, it speaks loud and clear. It demands that those who view it respect it. Vision stands out, and it never blends into the status quo. When spectators view the unfolding of someone else's vision, they will always conclude that the price to bring it to pass it too high for them to pay.

You will experience unspeakable joy whenever you witness what you once saw in your mind begin to take shape on the Earth. I have never known anyone's vision to manifest in the span of a week, a single month, or even one full year. It takes years for vision to rise from the ashes of thought in order to materialize in some concrete form. When you aggressively pursue your vision of tomorrow, you will achieve your goals and objectives along the way, all in the due incubation time for the birth of the baby you carry around in your minds eye. The Bible declares in Habakkuk 2:3 (NKJV):

> "For the vision [is] yet for an appointed time; But at the end it will speak, and it will not lie. Though it tarries, wait for it; because it will surely come, it will not tarry."

Make sure that you see your vision all the way through to fruition because it will not only benefit you, but countless others as well.

Tenacity is a Developed Attribute

TENACITY IS ONE OF THOSE RARE character traits that most people desire, but only a few display. It is synonymous with words such as perseverance, doggedness, persistence, clinging, and holding fast.

Contrary to popular opinion, tenacity is a developed trait; you can learn to be more tenacious in life. The problem, however, arises when we set out to acquire more of it. Tenacity lies dormant in all of us. It only surfaces when sparked by opposition or when forged in prolonged adversity. We observe it in operation in successful athletes, captains of industry, or in military leaders who win our respect by their unfailing commitment to succeed in the face of severe trial and testing.

> Acting the part does not mean that you are living the part.

Tenacity is not ours by birthright. It emerges because of one important ingredient…your *attitude*. Success and failure in life often hinges on your attitude in a given situation.

When small children crystallize in their minds an object of desire, they then become, to us older folks, the perfect embodiment of tenacity.

Their single-minded focus on obtaining one thing enables them to enjoy the fruit of their tenaciousness. If you have kids, you know what I mean…a house full of toys and gadgets you never intended to buy.

The same holds true with adults. The key to winning in life lies in your ability to focus long enough on a single goal or objective. Once you re-learn to do this (children do this instinctively), you will experience more success in all areas of your life. The ability to fix your attention on one goal at length is an ability that few people exercise. It is, however, an indispensable component of tenacity.

I recently watched a mixed martial arts fighting match where one fighter came into the ring wearing the meanest face you ever saw. He ground his teeth as though he were ready to eat his opponent. He screamed, yelled, and jumped around the ring, eager for the fight to start. He looked ferocious, to say the least. His opponent appeared tough, but calm. When the bell rang, the ferocious looking fighter ran toward his opponent and jumped in the air to kick him. Instead, he fell helplessly to the mat as a result of a well-placed kick from his calmer opponent. The match lasted just over a minute.

You Can't Fake Tenacity

Tenacity is a powerful component of the will that allows a person to endure unimaginable difficulty while maintaining a keen focus on victory. Acting the part does not mean that you are living the part. When reaching within to summon tenacity, remember a few points:

- Learn to press ahead regardless of the obstacles and struggles you are sure to encounter en route to accomplishing your goals.
- Stay with your program and see it through.
- Never become complacent with mediocrity when it is in you to deliver excellence.
- See your creation through to its completion, and do not stop until it looks exactly as you envisioned it.

Tenacity is a Developed Attribute

Although tenacity is a trait that is underdeveloped in most people, there are things you can do to cultivate it and tap its potential. Developing a more tenacious mindset can happen at any age…as long as you are prepared to make the mental adjustments required. The biggest key to becoming more tenacious is your refusal to give in to self-defeating assumptions and patterns of thought. If the challenges you face seem to have gotten the best of you, do not magnify them and assume you can never rebound from their assault. But remember…YOU WERE CREATED TO BOUNCE BACK FROM ALL ADVERSITY. Exemplify a bounce-back attitude, and before long, you will discover that tenacity is the weapon you have chosen to live without for far too long.

I Fought Three Tough Guys and Won

*C*HALLENGE, STRUGGLE, AND OPPOSITION—they are all a part of life's journey. These foundation-building ingredients are vital to any success you can ever hope to enjoy. You should never view them as unnecessary evils, placed in your path to derail your progress. The obstacles you encounter in life are there to shore up weak areas in your life. Facing and pressing through life's challenges is as necessary to your success as enjoying the prize for your efforts. I would dare argue that the challenges are more necessary to our success than the prizes at the end.

> The obstacles you encounter in life are there to shore up weak areas in your life.

The ripened fruit of perseverance is maturity. It blossoms as a result of successfully engaging in struggle in a particular area. And as you begin to mature, you will also experience a measure of confidence that attends the mastery of any skill. Whether in your personal or professional life, you must, at some point, come face to face with strong resistance or certain defeat. Challenges alone are the most trustworthy gauges of your weaknesses and strengths. Your crucibles will never lie to you about where you actually are in relation to where you ought to be in life.

Wanting to retreat from the heat of battle to the safety of your comfort zone is always tempting, but no one succeeds in capturing their dreams by playing it safe. Growth, in any venue of life, demands that you learn to fight through your feelings of fear of the unknown and disappointment with past setbacks.

> Wanting to retreat from the heat of battle to the safety of your comfort zone is always tempting.

As the pace of change in our world continues to accelerate, those unwilling to take risks in pursuit of their dreams or overcome challenges to obtain their goals will find that they are no longer relevant for the present, but relics of a bygone era. Individuals who consistently perform at peak levels possess certain common traits:

- An unwavering commitment to their success
- An uncommon passion for their profession
- Very clearly-defined goals

Individuals who possess these qualities are very comfortable taking calculated risks. In fact, their penchant for taking reasonable risks is indeed an important ingredient in their success and a noteworthy reason for it, as well. Risk taking is also a significant determinant in their level of achievement.

Top performers are talented and persistent risk-takers. They are not intimidated about meeting challenges head-on. In order to perform at the top of your game, you must develop a no-quit, can-do attitude. And you must become a passionate defender of those things about which you have strong core beliefs. Then, and only then, will you understand why I would rather enter the fray of battle than compromise on the quality of materials I use to build my tomorrows.

The One Mistake Most People Make

WHAT TYPE OF LIFESTYLE are you really interested in living? What do you want to accomplish with respect to your finances, marriage, or business? Are you willing to persevere in order to live the lifestyle you have been dreaming for so long, or are you simply looking to take the shortcut to success by hoping to win the lottery? Have you ever heard the old maxim, "If you continue to do the thing you've always done, you'll continue to get what you've always gotten"? How do you help someone who already knows what they are doing wrong but chooses not to make any behavior modifications?

These particular individuals can spell out all their shortcomings and even identify the reasons why they are not successful. One question, however, begs asking. If they are aware of the problems they continue to make, why then is there no strategy to

> Bad situations can change in the twinkling of an eye simply by drawing from the well of qualified help.

correct deficient behavior? One could wonder whether they are expecting change to fall from the sky, like manna.

Over the years, I have worked with many would-be millionaires. My observations lead me to conclude that these individuals cannot tell you how to achieve their financial goals because they have a faulty reference point—one that starts with faulty premises and points only in the direction of failure and not success. They are able to determine what actions they should take to get closer to their dreams, but they find it difficult to translate their understanding into concrete action. As a mentor and life coach to untold numbers of men and women across this country, my heart goes out to the many misguided individuals whose passions are mired in aimless effort.

The best remedy for stemming the tide of ruin in the wake of misdirected energy is the infusion of sound advice from a qualified mentor—one who can assist you with turning desire into productive, goal-achieving effort. For this to be effective, individuals must be painstakingly honest with themselves, and they must also be willing to adhere to sound counsel. Those who fall short of their goals in life must stop pretending to know what to do and openly admit a need for help. The longer you claim "I know" when you should be crying "I have no clue" the longer you hold your deliverance at bay.

Bad situations can change in the twinkling of an eye simply by drawing from the well of qualified help. Therefore, seek the advice of competent individuals who can point you in the right direction. Stop talking about what you are going to do and start doing what you have been talking about.

Procrastination: The Enemy of Success

PROCRASTINATORS ARE MADE, not born. Procrastination is learned indirectly in the family milieu and can be traced back to childhood. When children are not trained to be responsible for completing certain tasks in a determined timeframe, they are being groomed to procrastinate. When parents assign household chores to their children and hold them accountable for the timely completion of those responsibilities, parents are teaching their children the importance of completing tasks within allotted time constraints. As children mature, they take into adulthood what they learned at home, whether good or bad.

> Procrastinators actively look for distractions, particularly those that do not require much commitment on their part.

If parents permit their children to make excuses for failing to complete assigned chores, then they are encouraging their children to be irresponsible. Parents who choose not to hold their children to any standard of accountability do their precious loved ones a tremendous disservice.

According to various reputable studies, 20 percent of people identify themselves as chronic procrastinators. Sixty-seven percent of those same subjects studied fail to recognize that procrastination is a problem. In effect, they are too blind to see or admit that they carry around a persistent defect within that will rob them of productivity. Therefore, for them, procrastination is a normal part of life—albeit an antagonistic part—and they have no desire to rid themselves of this deficiency.

Procrastination can even be a form of rebellion. Procrastinators actively look for distractions, particularly those that do not require much commitment on their part. Sometimes, because of their fear of failure, they will intentionally procrastinate on a project so that their incompetence is masked, or explained away by unavoidable delays, stoppages, and setbacks. To the chronic procrastinator, productivity is always deferred to tomorrow, next time, or when conditions are more suited to getting things done. To the procrastinator, excuses abound—too many phone calls to answer…everybody wanting my time…or too much on my plate, etc.

Chronic procrastinators are usually chronic liars as well—liars in that falsehood (unjustified excuses) must be offered to mask inactivity. They are not necessarily bad people; they are simply people with a character flaw (to put it mildly). Nonetheless, there is a high cost for being a procrastinator and/or having one on your team or staff. Procrastinators can cost companies thousands; and depending on their position, they can even cost a company millions of dollars.

Imagine the price paid in your own life for taking action *later rather than now*. For example, have you ever gone to a department store and noticed that the shoes you have been eyeing for quite some time are now on sale for 75 percent off the ticketed price. Instead of pouncing on this great find, you procrastinate and decide to buy them the next day. But upon your return, you discover that your prized trophy has returned to its original price of $299. How costly was your delay?

Procrastination: The Enemy of Success

Instead of paying only $74.75, you are now out of pocket an extra $224.25 (the 75 percent off savings).

In a very real sense, everything in life boils down to dollars and cents. Therefore, you must understand that time truly is money. And time wasted is money lost forever. If you fail to structure your daily routine in a manner that respects time, your procrastination can lead to penury or dashed hopes, to say the least.

Would You Stand Out in a Group of 100 People?

How much does your perspective on life mirror that of the majority of people in this country? This may seem like a strange question to pose, but the truth implicit in your answer is telling. How unique do you believe yourself to be in comparison to others? Would you stand out in a crowd of, say, 100 other individuals? Would anyone notice your uniqueness or, in other words, your inherent value proposition? Or...would you blend into the tapestry of anonymous lives around you?

> The majority of people are more alike than they may care to admit.

- Out of every 100 individuals starting careers, twenty-nine of them are dead by age sixty-five.
- Sixty-eight percent of these same 100 individuals have an annual median income of $6,900.

- Only three out of every 100 people, or 3 percent, starting a career are actually financially successful—that is, having an annual income of over $41,500.

Imagine for a moment the implications of the above statistics. The majority of people are more alike than they may care to admit. These figures suggest that individuals have fallen into a rut that has become the beaten path. Without realizing what is actually happening, people settle effortlessly into the norm of their culture. As a result, they settle for biting off less of the American pie than they can actually chew.

The 3 percent of people considered financially successful, however, mirror the rest of the 100 folks when it comes to debt accumulation. Of the entire group of 100 career individuals, ninety-eight of them live month-to-month, under strapped conditions. They have mastered the practice of "running out of money before the end of the month." I, on the other hand, teach people how to position themselves financially to run out of month before they run out of money.

> You are the catalyst for improving your financial condition.

You are the catalyst for improving your financial condition. All of the investment goal setting, fiscal discipline, and budgeting that factor into a sound financial plan are your responsibility, and no one else's. Leaving these important matters to others to tend will leave you disappointed in the end.

I derive great joy and fulfillment as a life and business coach by helping scores of individuals to improve their lot in life. Nothing compares to the thrill I get whenever I witness the light turned on in the minds of my students, and they start to understand how to build wealth by becoming more productive in life—especially as their newfound prosperity is also a blessing to others.

I have noticed, however, that—despite all the wisdom I have and which has helped thousands of individuals—I have never been able to help anyone improve who is not first and foremost interested in becoming better or who does not cling to the possibility that life can get better.

Now is the time to invest in YOU by making the decision to attend my upcoming Dream Makers 99 Conclave titled "The Millionaire Wealth-Building Strategies." You are certain to reap untold benefit from the experience of being around other dreamers and from the wealth of information I provide to attendees. You will receive all the inspiration you need to believe that you can own, operate, and prosper abundantly with your own business. This event will help you to increase your bottom line with an existing business while providing others the impetus and the necessary tools and ideas to get a new business up and running.

At the risk of sounding like I am making a sales pitch, I can't stress enough the importance of the wisdom and information awaiting you at any of my Dream Makers 99 Conclaves. Success will manifest in your life from the information you receive and the encouragement you get—both of which I provide to my DM99 associates. So, endeavor to escape becoming a tragic financial statistic by planning your future on your terms. Allow me to reveal to you how to unlock the mystery of how to apply heaven's economic principles to your conditions here on Earth.

Five Great Lessons From a Pencil

PERFECTING YOUR CRAFT OR TALENT is not easy. It takes a lot of self-discipline and fortitude to fight through self-doubt and, perhaps, low self-esteem. There is an old maxim that says, "You are your own worst enemy." I say, "You are your greatest ally." You must accept the fact that you possess intrinsic value. Believing this may be difficult in light of the many challenges that seem only to underscore your weaknesses. However, you must also realize that if you have inherent weaknesses, you also possess some internal strengths.

There is one major reason why most people and businesses fail to reach their full potential. This particular reason is also the same root cause that undermines success in marriage, personal relationships, occupations, etc. The reason to which I am referring may come as a shock, but it originates from a failure to adhere to and apply information from a particular credible source. Hear the Parable of the Pencil:

> You can be your worst enemy or your best ally.

Unexpected Treasures

The Pencil Maker took the pencil aside, just before putting it into the box. "There are five things you need to know," he told the pencil, "before I send you out into the world. Always remember them and never forget, and you will become the best pencil you can be."

One: You will be able to do many great things, but only if you allow yourself to be held in someone else's hand.

Two: You will experience a painful sharpening from time to time, but you'll need it to become a better pencil.

Three: You will be able to correct any mistakes you might make.

Four: The most important part of you will always be what is inside.

Five: On every surface you are used, you must leave your mark. No matter what the condition, you must continue to write.

Asserting that he understood all and promising to remember all that had been said, the pencil entered the box with purpose in its heart. And like the pencil…

One: You will be able to do many great things, but only if you allow yourself to be held in God's hand. Moreover, you must find competent teachers and mentors to help you to access the many gifts you possess.

Two: You too will experience the pain that accompanies being sharpened by the refining trials of life. Though painful, you will need them to become a stronger person.

Three: Like the pencil, you will undoubtedly make mistakes in life that are never so indelible that God's forgiveness cannot erase them.

Five Great Lessons From a Pencil

Four: As you comprehend the possibilities of your greatness, you will discover that the most important part of you will always be what is on the inside.

Five: Everywhere you travel, you must leave your mark. No matter the situation, you must continue to live out your design and purpose.

By understanding and remembering all that was said here, you must journey through life with full assurance that there is purpose in your heart—purpose that will cause you to leave behind great things for us to discover.

Living with the
Fear of Challenge

WHEN IT COMES TO PURSUING what you believe you are capable of achieving, why do you hesitate? Even worse, why do you allow negative thoughts to commandeer your focus? Why must you surrender the high ground of positive thinking to the guttural thought of failure? Why is it that when you reach for success, you shrink back believing that you are going to be handed failure, instead? Is it fair to demand so little of yourself when you know within your heart of hearts that you are capable of enjoying so much more?

The answers to these questions are really quite simple. In general, people earnestly desire to live better than they currently live. We all wish to fulfill our dreams. Owning a business and finishing college are important goals to many people. Unfortunately, fear paralyzes most people before they can even set sail on their journeys. While most people

> The longer you sit around hoping that your financial situation will change, the longer you will sit around doing nothing.

Unexpected Treasures

want success, they do not want the struggle that goes along with it. However, this is one fact of life we must all face.

With every ounce of success you enjoy in life, you will also taste a corresponding measure of struggle. Because of this reality, many shy away from making that maiden voyage that will launch their dreams. As a result, fear gives way to procrastination, which ultimately stalls the birth of the success you may have dreamt for so long.

Allowing fear to control your thoughts is very crippling. It will keep you from venturing down paths in life where challenges and setbacks are sure to be lurking. Fear will even cause you to give strength to invisible opponents. Yes, fear is a powerful obstacle, when we give it life.

Imagine, though, what you could accomplish if fear were not that looming albatross, hovering over your life. Think how different your life would be without the resistance of fear in it. When faced with challenges, always ask yourself, "What additional problems do I create by not addressing the issues at hand?" Burying your head in the sand will not cause your problems to disappear; such action will only compound the nature of your difficulties.

The longer you sit around hoping that your financial situation will change, the longer you will sit around doing nothing. Complaining about what you don't have or what you can't do will not change your circumstances in the least. The only thing that will change a bad situation is better effort applied to it. Do not be afraid to apply better solutions to your current situation.

Therefore, tackle your fears so you can begin to destroy any procrastination that may be holding you back. In the end, your rewards will be great and the opposition overcome will strengthen your character.

You Are Incredible

PSYCHOLOGISTS CLAIM THAT THE number one problem that constantly plagues most people is an image of low self-esteem. Do people actually spend so much time struggling with their worth and value? The craze today in our society is plastic surgeries of all types, and this phenomenon underscores the fact that people generally do not like what they see in the mirror. We put so much stock on outward appearance but spend very little time tending to the inner self.

I truly believe that we would all be much more balanced in life if we would devote only 10 percent of our efforts toward renovating the exterior and direct 90 percent of our energies on our internal makeup. Just because our house may look immaculate on the outside, does not mean that the inside is a mirror image. Indeed, it often is not. Unfortunately, we do not live outside our homes, where pretenses are easier to keep up.

> Understand that you are the only one who can actually determine the most accurate market value for your life.

A healthy self-esteem begins on the inside. Until the inside of your house is swept, cleaned and put in order, you will never properly appraise the value of the exterior. If you place all your stock on the exterior, your self-esteem will always suffer an unhealthy assessment.

The vagaries of life can transform us in an instant and in ways we can scarcely imagine or brace for. A sudden automobile accident or a devastating illness can render us deformed beyond recognition. If you invest all of your worth in the superficial exterior, what then becomes of your self-worth when your physical appearance no longer meets with your approval? Do you still move forward in life or do you begin to wither on the vine at that moment.

Chance will ensure that we all experience our fair share of setbacks. However, they do not have to incapacitate us. It behooves us to reprioritize the focus we place on external and internal matters. Investing now to increase the stability of spiritual and emotional aspects of your life will ensure that, when the unfortunate happens, you will be able to stand to face the winds when they blow fiercely, trying to separate you from your foundation.

Please, do not misunderstand the point I am trying to make. Giving attention to how we appear on the outside is very important, because our outward looks are the cover by which others make their initial judgments. Therefore, it only makes good sense to ensure that we present the best image possible. But...

The problem exists when we place all of our worth on what is only apparent to natural eyes. Deep within the fiber of your being are qualities that you should be nurturing more than the physical attributes.

Understand that you are the only one who can actually determine the most accurate market value for your life. Others can only guess based on what they see on the outside. Only you know the abundant reservoir of treasures locked away inside your being. If you choose to focus only on the superficial aspects of who you are, you will never take time to explore the more important inner terrain of your being—where all your true treasures and wealth exist. The last place most people look to find their wealth is actually the first place they should begin their search. Dreams, inventions, and great ideas are all harvested within you, not outside you.

While it may be true that feelings of low self-esteem are the number one issue that affects most people, you no longer have to be part of this group, if you currently are. You determine how you feel about yourself, no one else can. When you discover what is most important in life, I am certain you will also find that the most important things in life gravitate to unseen qualities. You cannot purchase true love, contentment, serenity, and fulfillment with material things. We can only secure them by what we find after we discover self. Oftentimes that journey takes most of a lifetime simply to begin…but begin it must.

Therefore, change the way you feel about yourself by changing what you do or who you go to for validation. Begin by spending more time renovating your inside than the outside. Once you do, a wonderful thing will begin to happen. The outside of your house will begin to take on a higher appraised value in your own estimation, as well as in the eyes of others.

Consider the following excerpt from an inspiring poem by Marianne Williamson titled "Our Great Fear."

> *Our deepest fear is not that we are inadequate. Our deepest fear is that we are powerful beyond measure. It is our light not our darkness that most frightens us. We ask ourselves, who am I to be brilliant, gorgeous, talented and fabulous?*

Our true fear—the thing holding us back—is that we can achieve all that we put our minds to accomplish. We simply place fear in front of us to have an excuse for failure. Remove the excuse by removing the fear by believing in Incredible YOU.

Education Does Not Guarantee Success

HAVE YOU EVER NOTICED that the most academically gifted among us are usually not the ones who make it the furthest in life?

While an academic environment may teach one how to learn and assimilate information, it does not teach one how to succeed in life. In general, schools teach you facts, things that are or have been. At school, the student's focus is on accumulating and recalling information. Tests measure a student's ability to retain and regurgitate information. Consequently, if a student does well at information recall, he or she will, in all likelihood, become an academic success.

As these academic studs enter the job market, they do tend to earn a wage or salary that is, on average, higher than that of their peers. In this regard, their past academic achievements qualify them for higher financial compensation. However, academic achievement is not a reliable indicator of entrepreneurial success in life—success that is

> Man is the only one of God's creations dependent on money for a living.

based on a certain level of risk taking. Typically, the most gifted academicians and perfectionists are risk averse. Therefore, they tend not to venture into the realm of the unknown, where all the lucrative possibilities exist.

Over 95 percent of the world's wealthiest individuals admit that they abandoned their academic pursuits in order to follow some sort of business passion that going to school would not accommodate. These business mavericks all agree that, though important for most, conventional learning was not their thing. Success in their arena would require certain qualities that the classroom simply could not teach. Consequently, formal education became an obstacle to acquiring the required tools of the trade.

Is one person better than another simply because of his higher earning power? Of course not! Jesus never glorified poverty; neither did He ever criticize the legitimate earning of wealth. God made all things for our use and enjoyment, including food, clothing, and precious metals. God has declared that all things He has made are good (Gen. 1:31).

God certainly knows the things we need in order to live (Matt. 6:32). Material wealth often gives the owner a dangerously false sense of security, one that often ends in tragedy. The birds of the air and the lilies of the field neither fret with toil nor worry where they will live, yet they enjoy God's wealth in ways that man cannot duplicate. All of nature depends on God, and He has never failed His creation at any time. Man is the only one of God's creations dependent on money for a living. And it's strange just how often money fails us, given that we are supposed to be the most intelligent of His created beings.

Keep in mind what Paul warned about money in saying, "that the love of money is the root of all evil." However, money itself possesses no intrinsic moral quality of good or evil. Any good or bad that results from the money we have is conveyed by the owners of it.

Therefore, understand that academic success does not often translate to financial success. You are the only one who can determine whether your life is a financial success or not. You must measure the financial rewards you currently enjoy against what your gifts, talents, and purpose in life dictate that you should be earning. If the gap is wide, work to shorten it.

The Death of Dysfunction

DYSFUNCTION IS A WORD that suggests a failure in the functioning of a particular thing or a disturbance in its usual pattern of activity. In other words, where dysfunction occurs, there exists a breakdown in the standard operating system with respect to some entity or system, whether it is a person, family, business, or machine.

We live a world filled with chaos and disorder. Dysfunction exists all around us. What family unit is not dysfunctional, on some level? What business does not suffer, to some degree, from the ravages of inefficient operations? Despite our best efforts, dysfunction will, sooner or later, attempt to attach itself to any and every facet of our lives. Once dysfunction takes root, it takes determined commitment to kill it.

> Once dysfunction takes root, it takes determined commitment to kill it.

That said, how do we manage in the face of the plethora of dysfunction all around? How do we account for all the productivity that is lost due to dysfunction?

As suggested earlier, dysfunction results from an absence of functionality. Therefore, dysfunction steps out of the shadows to become a surrogate standard, in the absence of an enforced one. Our ignorance of certain standards or our unwillingness to enforce them becomes sufficient opportunity for dysfunction to gain a foothold in our daily lives.

Because dysfunction creeps in rather gradually, we are often unaware that it is even present. As things around us begin to change slowly for the worse, we make mental adjustments to our new environment. Before long, we awake to a new status quo that is entirely unrecognizable to the original standard.

The failure to recognize the subtle changes to our environment is, perhaps, the biggest culprit in the onset of dysfunctional situations, wherever they exist. Once one standard gets relaxed, others become minor technicalities that are then easily compromised. Over time, this domino effect can render a person, a family, or an organization without a framework sufficient to support its main mission. When so much of an organization's operating policies are compromised, those with eyes to see the poor state of affairs often feel powerless to do anything about the decay.

Enforcing high standards, in all honesty, requires tremendous vigilance and effort. In most cases, people have never been taught the importance of living by and enforcing standards. This is where an effective mentor or life coach is worth his or her weight in gold. Capable mentors can quickly recognize where you are cutting corners in life, thereby setting yourself up for future trouble. They can also show you where you are in life versus where you should be. Most importantly, they can pinpoint areas in your life where dysfunctional behavior and thinking are undermining your efforts.

Think about this for a moment. God never intended marriage to be a combat zone when He first gave the institution to man. However, that is what it has become for millions in this country. Neither were people supposed to live below their potential as a result of self-imposed financial limitations. These are just two common areas of life where our belief systems easily break down and fail to function according to God's design.

The Death of Dysfunction

If a person does not live according to a set of standards of his choosing, other people will take delight in imposing theirs upon that individual. Ask the millions of men and women in prisons all across this country.

Proper functioning, in any area, typically precedes dysfunction. For instance, individuals enter marriage with every intention of making it work. In the beginning, things function properly, as anticipated. Over time, however, individuals begin to cut corners; they start to violate certain principles; and they soon replace healthy respect for the other with overall disregard. What results is marital dysfunction.

In order to overcome the dysfunction that hampers progress in any system, identify the principles that govern the thing you wish to operate, whether it is a marriage, raising children, a job, or running a business. Principles undergird everything in life. Knowing which ones govern certain undertakings will cause life to run smoothly...when followed.

> Principles undergird everything in life.

Is Your Life Good?

THANKSGIVING, CHRISTMAS AND the New Year are times for reflection and introspection. People often say that life is good, but life is what you make of it as a direct result of the opportunities God extends to you. We put life in crystal-clear perspective when we focus our attention on the Creator rather than on His creation.

When I stop to ponder how far God has brought me, I can only conclude… God is good. I do not need to compare my life with anyone else's to arrive at this conclusion. I am the perfect fit for everything God has destined for me, be it fortune or times of great testing. I have learned over the years that God equips us to handle the circumstances He sends our way. He qualifies us to receive His priceless blessings, and He tries us to increase our capacity to produce yet more in life—all for His glory.

In my many struggles, God has been my ever-present help in time of need. He has brought me through every trial by giving me surpassing

> I have learned over the years that God equips us to handle the circumstances.

victories on more occasions than I care to imagine. In my weakest hours, God has always supplied the strength I needed to go on. When, at times, I have suffered hunger, God provided food for me to enjoy. When I have experienced unspeakable loneliness, He proved to be a faithful comforter and companion. I could go on and on listing the many adversities I have experienced, but I could also produce a list just as long, detailing God's guiding hand through every struggle I have ever encountered.

God's hand of deliverance has been too awesome to describe and too numerous to recount. In the end, I am left to conclude that there is nothing too hard for God.

The financial success I enjoy today is a direct result of God's providential blessings poured out over my life. However, they did not come without a price. I enjoy what I do today because I decided to make His plan for me my sole mission in life. Because I chose long ago to surrender my life to His will, I discovered that God takes it upon Himself to supply me with sufficient strength, knowledge, and wisdom to fulfill His purpose for me on Earth. Therefore, all praise must go to Jesus Christ for all the success I have enjoyed to this present hour. He is the Author and Finisher of my faith…

May you know Him as yours!

Take Control of Your Life!

WHO IS AT THE HELM of your life? This is a serious question! Most people are looking for someone else to tell them what to do, how to do it, and even when to do it. Initiative is the operative word when it comes to taking back the controls of your life. Just think about how much control has been lost where your money is concerned. What is the present state of your family? What is your debt structure like? Do you have a plan in place that will help get your life back on track?

Consumer spending tends to grow much faster than the rate of income received. The average American household suffers under the weight of more than $10,000 in credit card debt. We have made debt part of our everyday lifestyle. With the state of the today's economy, debt should be the last thing you go shopping for.

> With the state of the today's economy, debt should be the last thing you go shopping for.

Unexpected Treasures

Consider the increasing divorce epidemic sweeping across our nation. The staggering number of failed marriages experienced annually in this nation contributes greatly to our economic crisis. Gambling addictions often begin with a win it all to fix it all approach to dealing with financial crisis…only to realize that gambling, in all of its ugly manifestations, is generally a big waste of precious time and money. Staggering gambling losses are an additional contributing factor to the problems in our economy.

If I were to offer one bit of advice to the American public, it would be…TAKE CONTROL OF YOUR LIFE!

Each New Year is an opportunity to take back the controls of more of your life. If there are areas in your life where you have lost control, make a firm commitment this year to take back control. Make a pledge to yourself that you will again be the captain of your destiny. With this renewed affirmation, locate the tools to help you deal with debt, a struggling marriage, or a battle with low self-esteem. Get serious about acquiring the right information to stay on course and properly assess your progress.

Join me and thousands of others around the country as we get the necessary information to take back control of our lives. Many of my personal published materials offer a great starting point to accomplish this. I would strongly recommend that you read my book *Building Wealth from the Ground Up* together with the accompanying *Building Wealth from the Ground Up Workout Material*. Trust me when I say the cost is minimal but the control you will gain is priceless.

Getting Out of Debt? Hogwash

IS IT POSSIBLE TO GET COMPLETELY out of debt? Indeed, it is. But, is it a realistic goal to set? Considering the culture we live in today, it is next to impossible to live without debt of some sort, unless you are a person of sufficient financial means who is able to make expensive purchases without having to pull out the plastic. Debt reduction is actually a more realistic objective for most Americans than getting completely out of debt, especially if you are between the ages of eighteen and sixty-five.

Ninety-eight percent of all Americans between the ages eighteen to sixty-five are just entering the job market, building a career, or preparing for retirement. Additionally, 95 percent of a person's assets and liabilities are acquired between these ages. Unless you have a sizeable trust fund waiting for you at age eighteen, you are most likely going to fall into the debt trap, once you embark on life out from under the protection of your parents.

> Keep in mind that debt builds just as wealth does...over time.

Unexpected Treasures

Certain major purchases like a car, college tuition, or a home will almost certainly make debt necessary, for most.

Most people do not have the kind of savings account established where they can withdraw $150,000 for the purchase of a new house. Therefore, debt reduction, rather than elimination, should be your first objective when it comes to improving your financial well-being. This does not mean that you should not aim for total eradication of your debt. It simply means that you may want to lower you initial sights in order to conquer the smaller giants before taking on Goliath, metaphorically speaking.

A young man once asked me how long it would take him to get out of debt. I followed his question with one of my own. I then asked him, "How much disposable income do you have remaining after paying your monthly expenses?"

In all truth, if you come up short or have very little money remaining after paying your bills, then getting out of debt can take quite some time. However, if you have a surplus of, say, $500 or more remaining after satisfying your monthly obligations, getting out of debt becomes a much quicker possibility. The key, though, is in knowing which debts to attack first, taking into consideration such factors as interest rates, current balances, and time until each debt obligation expires.

Keep in mind that debt builds just as wealth does…over time. As with building any kind of wealth, you must learn to utilize the element of time as a crucial weapon in your battle against debt.

Become better informed. If possible, seek the advice of a qualified financial planner, whether you feel you can afford one or not. Their consultation services are free, in most cases. Furthermore, they can provide you with a comprehensive assessment of your financial fitness as well as with a game plan for becoming debt-free.

Hidden Money

MOST PEOPLE STRUGGLE WITH MONEY because they do not quite understand its true nature. They may have some sense of money's value when it comes to allowing them to purchase goods and services. In general, people fail to appreciate the powerful potential that is stored inside the currency they carry around every day.

Aptly defined, money is a (1) store of value, (2) a measure of value, and (3) a medium of exchange. Additionally, money allows us to transport power—spending power—wherever we go and to convey that power to whomever we choose. It facilitates exchange in society in ways that barter systems never could.

Most people regard money only as that thing we labor hard to obtain and take pleasure in spending. However, money is more than an illusive device with wings. Furthermore, it does more than enable us to feed our consumer demands. If you always look to spend the money you make, you will never have any of it for your future enjoyment. Unfortunately, this is the plight of most Americans.

> Money is more than an elusive device with wings.

Unexpected Treasures

When a person narrowly regards money only for the spending power it provides, that individual typically takes little notice of how much of it he or she routinely wastes on unnecessary things. On the other hand, wealthy individuals tend to possess healthy respect for the money they earn. They also realize that money works better as a servant in the economy than as master over their lives.

People who have built fortunes through their creative efforts have discovered money's hidden potential. They unlock the full potential of money by understanding and applying its many purposes.

When you do not know the purpose of money, you will abuse it. Therefore, debt and financial hardships will tend to follow you throughout life. Learning to make money work for you, instead of you slaving for it, is the first step to mastering it.

Some people become filled with rage when they see others amass great fortunes, seemingly without much effort. You too can amass more wealth if you know where you have hidden it. Allow me to repeat myself. You can enjoy having more money if you would simply identify where you are wasting it. Once you plug the holes, your savings will begin to grow.

You do not need a raise from your boss in order to locate additional funds. What you need is the knowledge to unlock the door to the wealth you already have.

Most people have significant sums of money hidden in wasteful or unnecessary behavior. For example, you may be spending substantial amounts of money on monthly services you do not use or need. Perhaps you may be paying for a premium package cable service, but you routinely only watch the basic channels. Consider your mobile phone service. Do you really need all the features you are currently paying for? If not, eliminate some unnecessary features and enjoy the savings. When you stop to consider the many things we do that waste money, you will quickly realize that you and I have more hidden money that we may care to admit.

Therefore, the key is not necessarily in working to obtain more money but in locating where much of our money currently hides. Once you find it, sit back and watch the mountain begin to grow.

Achieving Success without Regret

"I have learned that if one advances confidently in the direction of his dreams, and endeavors to live the life he has imagined, he will meet with a success unexpected in common hours."
—Henry David Thoreau

WE INVARIABLY ENCOUNTER OBSTACLES and setbacks as we move toward our desires in life. Most, however, mistake them as a sure sign they are going in the wrong direction. Nothing could be further from the truth. Obstacles are a part of life's challenges. If it were easy to achieve success, then more people would venture down the path that leads to their dreams.

In reality, achieving success is a very trying proposition—whatever the pursuit. Whether you are attempting to lose weight or gain financial freedom, you are going to face opposition at every turn. In all actuality, overcoming the obstacles

> Pursue your dreams this year with all the fortitude you can muster.

en route to your final destination is oftentimes more rewarding than reaching the goal itself. The thrill of obtaining the prize is often short-lived in comparison to the satisfaction you will experience by overcoming the difficulty getting there.

When interviewed, retired athletes are often asked what they miss most about the sport they once played. Nearly all of them share that they miss most the physical and mental preparation needed to perform at that level as much as winning the rewards that go along with victory.

Fighting with a determination to win in life requires just as much commitment as fighting to win in any sport. However, the stakes are much higher in real life. Additionally, the opponents we face in life are more relentless in pressing their attacks; they know no bell. Yet, they must eventually surrender to your persistent endeavor to move forward in the direction of your dreams.

Pursue your dreams this year with all the fortitude you can muster. Despite the false starts or the setbacks of the previous year, set out this year with only one goal in mind…a staunch determination to begin and stay the course of your journey.

With one year already behind you and another in your future, you are at a critical fork in the road. Will you stall in your tracks, harping on the things of the past? Or, will you reach for the promise of your tomorrows? Ask God for the strength to face life's challenges. Remember… your best days are yet ahead of you.

Watch Your Attitude

How do you maintain a healthy mental attitude when life seems to spin out of control? Have you learned to anchor your optimism in a hopeful outlook of your future, or do you allow your thoughts to fall victim to the whims of your circumstances?

Your mental attitude always ventures toward that proverbial fork in the road—always struggling whether to go right or left. Taking possession of our minds and guiding them to whatever ends we choose is the one thing we can do to help ensure our success or guarantee our peace of mind, while experiencing life's challenges.

> Your attitude is the ruler that determines how far you are willing to go in life.

Napoleon Hill once said:

> *Mental attitude is a determining factor—perhaps the most important one—of what results one gets from prayer. Only prayers that are backed by a mental attitude of profound faith can be expected to bring positive results.*

Unexpected Treasures

People often allow situations to control their mental attitudes rather than learning to maintain an even keel in the midst of changing circumstances. Once surrendered to circumstances, it is difficult to reel in wayward thoughts and emotions. If you do not learn to control your mental attitude, someone or something else will step into the void and begin dictating terms for you. When this happens, panic, fear, and confusion often results, as we realize how little control we are left holding.

Though you may not be able to control every situation you confront, you can take possession of your mind to ensure the best outcome possible for you.

We go through three stages whenever we encounter problems. The three stages are:

1. How you view yourself going in. (past)
2. How you view yourself while in it. (present)
3. How you view yourself coming out. (future)

In truth, you are the only one who can determine the state of your mental attitude. You can blame situations, and you can even blame others for how you react to external events. But, at the end of the day, you still have ownership of your mind. Look at yourself in the mirror and ask yourself, "Would I want to be in a life and death situation with the power of choice in my hands?" How you respond to this question reveals plenty about you. Hesitation on your part may expose a lack of confidence in yourself.

In order to have a healthy mental attitude, you must ensure that you possess a healthy dose of self-confidence, so that you never empower anyone else to make decisions for you.

Understanding Yourself

How honest are you with yourself? Are you the kind of person who sees no wrong in what you do but can see vividly all the wrong in others? If you were stranded on a deserted island with just one other person, would you want that other person to be someone like you? Would you choose instead to be marooned with your spouse, a friend, or even a favorite pet? We all have preferred relationships, although we may not always be so free to admit it. Honesty can teach us much about ourselves.

Are you prepared to embark on a journey to discover more about yourself—to learn your likes and dislikes, your strengths and weaknesses, and your sources of comfort and fear? Understanding yourself is the first step in the process of determining what kind of

> Honesty can teach us much about ourselves.

person you actually are as opposed to the type person you think you are. It is important that you are comfortable exploring your inner workings.

In sales, success is measured in contract closings and money collected. During an actual sales session, progress is determined by how close the salesperson gets to having the customer sign on the dotted line. The more progress you make in the process, the closer you are to landing the sale. Every salesperson knows that product knowledge is vital to establishing credibility with customers.

The same holds true with you. You are your own best product. No one should know you better than you know yourself. The more transparent you are in your study of self, the more progress you will make in closing the deal on bringing home your ideal self.

The key to having fulfilling relationships with God and others is to know yourself intimately. Jesus said that the second of the two greatest commandments is to "love your neighbor as you love yourself." Here Jesus states that we should love ourselves with a kind of love that would suggest an intimate knowledge of who we are. When you truly love anyone, there exists some level of intimate knowledge regarding that individual. Therefore, you must endeavor to learn as much as you can about yourself so that you can truly love yourself, if you do not already.

Having set out on the path of self-discovery, you must be prepared to answer the following questions:

- What are you looking for in life? and Why?
- What value do you add to others that they should be drawn to you?
- What do you like and dislike about yourself?
- What is your greatest strength?
- What is your greatest weakness?

These are only five questions that will help you probe your inner being. They represent the kind of probing questions you should explore as you go through a process of self-discovery. Once you have answered these kinds of questions honestly, you will then have a good understanding of who you actually are.

The Secrets to Success

IN TODAY'S HECTIC MARKETPLACE, we all get inundated with news headlines, advertisements, and books that claim to be able to reveal the secrets of the rich and famous. The staggering sale of merchandise that promises to expose the hidden mysteries of celebrities and society jet-setters suggests that the majority of people take their cues from a very small group of individuals. But what do these famous and wealthy individuals have that most people do not?

Having studied carefully the issue of success in all its many forms, I have always been amazed at how ordinary the wealthy actually are. Individuals who enjoy phenomenal wealth and fame possess no special anointing to do what they do. I have discovered that principles are all that separate successful people from unsuccessful individuals. That alone is the key.

Like most, I used to believe that wealth was an elusive notion and that rich people were given some special endowment at birth. Are some

> Acquiring money is among the least rewarding aspects of true success.

people more likely to succeed than others? Is there a secret place the wealthy go to gain exposure to highly classified success secrets? We have all asked ourselves these kinds of questions at some point in life, especially if we are not one of the fortunate few to have wealth or fame.

I no longer believe that obtaining success is a mystery. I believe that most people know what to do to succeed, but they simply allow fear and laziness to deny them the better things in life. Besides, each of us must define success based on our unique purpose in life. Making money and acquiring fame are not all there is to success. In fact, they are the least of the ingredients.

Acquiring money is among the least rewarding aspects of success. Many people make substantial incomes at jobs they hate. Therefore, making money does not define success. You find success when you discover the one thing that brings out your passion for living. Once you find that profession, you then will enjoy personal fulfillment. This is what most wealthy individuals know all too well. They labor in life to do the thing that brings them fulfillment. They are not afraid to pay the price to chase a dream or enjoy their heart's desire.

You can still pursue your passion, even though you may still work a nine-to-five job. The bottom-line is that you just need to start going after the things that ignite your passion and bring you personal fulfillment. There is no rush to leave the safety of your job until you are comfortable doing so. However, do not allow your job to keep you from pursuing your dreams—a proposition frightening to most individuals.

If you would cast your fears aside to chase your destiny, you will soon find yourself in that upper echelon of successful individuals, with the masses wanting to know what special endowments God gave you. However, you will know the truth…that success comes to anyone who chooses to live according to certain principles rather than by certain fears.

World Shaper or Moneymaker?

ARE YOU AN ASSET or a liability? Allow me to rephrase the question. Do those you know consider you an asset or a liability? Have you committed your full energies to ensuring the growth of your church, business, employer, or family...in ways that would positively impact your community? What is the estimate of your overall benefit to others? This is the ultimate question.

When I examine how a person conducts his or her daily affairs, I can tell right away whether that individual is a world shaper or simply a moneymaker. There is a huge difference between the two types of individuals. Moneymakers are only interested in building careers and making as much money as possible. Personal and professional relationships are important only so far as they further those two goals. On the other hand, world shapers look to improve the plight of their fellow man at their own expense of money, time, energy, and entrepreneurship.

> The answer is that money can never do for the human heart what serving others alone does.

In the Bible, the Apostle Paul said, "If we live only to ourselves we are men most miserable." In effect, Paul is declaring that we will be left unfulfilled if our pursuits in life are only self-directed. As people, we find meaning in what we do for others. Serving others, therefore, is the most rewarding occupation of time you can ever experience.

The majority of people search for personal fulfillment in all the wrong places. You will not discover it in a job, if that job does not somehow allow you to serve others. Most people set out in life to pursue a career that will net them the most money possible. After a short while, they wonder why they are not content with the job they have. The answer is that money can never do for the human heart what serving others alone does. Making money is a shallow investment of time when it comes to seeking personal fulfillment.

I have chosen to dedicate myself to a life of service that does not hold out the promise of lucrative gain. As a life and business coach, however, my reward often comes in the form of personal satisfaction from helping others. Though my personal sacrifices are many, more are the joys of personal fulfillment I experience daily. Helping others through my mentoring and coaching is 'thank you' enough.

My role as a life and business coach, however, in no way prevents me from pursuing wealth in other business ventures. In fact, I believe in creating multiple streams of income to increase the chances for money to find its way into my life. My goal is to maximize my talents and abilities in order to attract the most amount of money I can in order to fulfill the mandate on my life.

Indeed, my life attracts wealth because I am dedicated to the lives of others. I do not serve money; I serve God and people. I strongly believe that we can never measure service to God and others in dollars and cents. I believe the number one reason why most people fail to answer God's call on their lives is the fear of what they would have to surrender in the process. Like the rich young ruler who walked away from Jesus sorrowful, most people believe that God would require them to give up all they possess to follow Him, leaving them destitute in exchange. Nothing could be further from the truth.

What God endeavors to do is to realign our priorities, so that money does not become our master. Jesus once said, "Man cannot serve both God and money…" If you cannot give it freely when God asks for it, then you do not own it; it owns you. Live a life of service to God and man, and God will fill your life with the true treasures that only He can provide.

Working like a slave to make money is rarely, if ever, the answer to becoming wealthy. On the other hand, stories abound with how individuals became wealthy by simply addressing the needs of their fellow man. Therefore, find the joy of serving others with your whole heart so that money will become your servant.

Discover Your Passion
37

ARE YOU LIVING YOUR PASSION? Have you committed to developing a winning strategy to cultivate greatness? No person can reach his or her full capacity without being committed to achieving it. Never measure your success against an idealistic standard of perfection. Instead, measure your success by the progress you make in pursuit of clearly defined, measurable, and challenging goals.

Settle on realistic goals based on your passion. Avoid setting goals you can easily achieve, and do not place them so far out of reach that they are impossible to reach. Believable goals are far better to pursue than inconceivable ones.

What is it that causes an athlete to perform at his or her best? What motivates a scoring champion to kick into overdrive in the last few minutes of a game to bring his team back from the brink of defeat? What enables a boxer to endure extreme physical abuses in the ring, round after round… and then find the wherewithal to knock out his opponent with one crashing blow. The answer to all the above questions is *passion*.

> Passion is the key to succeeding in life.

Unexpected Treasures

Oftentimes, people want to achieve success at bargain basement prices without investing their time, energy, and resources. My friend, you must discover the things you value most in life because protecting, securing, and nurturing them will unleash the fight in you when they are threatened. You will fight to succeed in life when you know that realizing your dream will feed precious loved ones and free them from their despair.

Passion is the key to succeeding in life. Do not aim for greatness without it. Your success is inevitable when you couple passion with the goal of reaching a dream. It provides the staying power to face and overcome your obstacles.

Regardless of how often you hear others talk about our dreadful economy, alarming divorce rates, and staggering unemployment, do not allow these pessimists to rain on your parade. Continue to fight to enjoy a wonderful marriage, a successful business, or simply a very fulfilling life. If you can discover your passion for living, it will soon spill over into other areas of your life as well. It truly is your calling card to success and dream fulfillment in any area of life.

Legacy! What is Yours?

WHEN THE LAST CHAPTER of your life has been read and the book cover is closed, will most people feel that you never got the opportunity to experience your full potential? Will they conclude that you denied countless others the opportunity to gain from your wisdom? Will they believe that you robbed future generations of the wealth of resources and courageous tales you never left behind?

It is supposed to be that the enlightenment and discovery of previous generations should become commonplace understanding for subsequent ones.

> The wealthiest place on earth is in the most unlikely place—the graveyard.

Our accumulation of wisdom, understanding, and experiences must enable the next generation to avoid the pitfalls of our time and allow them to benefit from its accomplishments. We leave legacies to our children so that they can experience and treasure the passion and tenor of the past.

Unexpected Treasures

I discovered long ago that the richest place in the world is not the United States; it is not Saudi Arabia; and it certainly is not Hollywood (Beverly Hills). The wealthiest place on Earth is in the most unlikely place—the graveyard. More wealth is secured in a small six-foot by three-foot plot of land than in the greatest oil producing countries in the world. Once we lay to rest the deceased's wealth of knowledge and wisdom, there is no way ever again to unlock that treasure chest. The wealth that body once contained is forever lost, and the world must suffer the void of that individual's contribution to humanity.

The late Dr. Turnel Nelson was my greatest mentor. I loved and revered this man greatly. He was the pastor of a thriving ministry in Trinidad, and he also served as a mentor to many other pastors around the world. He embraced me as a son, and unlocked in me more understanding than I ever thought I had. To this day, I still benefit from the multi-faceted potential that Dr. Nelson caused me to discover so many years ago. He poured himself out to countless leaders across the globe. What a tremendous legacy he left behind! He would often say, "Don't die full!"

The fruit that grows from the tree of your life experiences will leave behind precious seeds for future generations to germinate. Growing older does not mean you have to stop growing and enjoying life. In fact, growing older should suggest the opposite. The longer I am on this Earth, the more fruit I get to grow, and the more seeds I get to scatter for those whom I influence.

There is a Champion in You

IT IS TIME FOR YOU TO ARISE and begin living the kind of life you were destined to enjoy. Your biggest challenge in life is not an external opponent but the one within. The greatest obstacle to your success is the mountain of self-doubt you carry around ever day; conquer it and you will win more than half the battles you are guaranteed to encounter in life. If not, discouragement will give way to apathy, which will in turn surrender ground to a series of failed attempts at everything you do.

As you reach for more in life, there will come a time when you will have to dig deep in order to locate the champion within you. Greatness is the constant companion of those with the courage to court it, not of those too timid to express interest. The closer you get to victory in any area, the greater is the sacrifice required along the way. You will find that the effort you

> As you reach for more in life, there will come a time when you will have to dig deep in order to locate the champion within you.

once exerted to perform certain tasks is insufficient to meet the current demands. What an awakening to discover that yesterday's strength, desire, and passion are not sufficient to secure tomorrow's victories. Understand that opposition is a natural part of life.

Failure is a part of Success

You must never be afraid to fail, and do not waste time trying to build into your plans fail-safe systems to avoid it. Learn from your failures and go on to the next challenge. It is okay to fail, but it is never okay to stay down after failure strikes. If you are not experiencing some measure of failure in life, you are not growing. After all, failure is the barometer that lets us know when mid-course corrections are necessary.

The challenge of change is always hard, at first. However, it is important that you begin to confront the change that challenges you, so you can take the lead in shaping your own future. Although failure was never wired into our creative design, it has become necessary for our continued growth, ever since the fall of Adam in the Garden of Eden. Failure is simply an indication that you have not gone far enough, searched deep enough, stayed long enough or sacrificed enough for the sake of discovering that unimaginable treasure within you.

Danger: Comfort Zone Ahead

Most people, after arriving at a certain level of wealth and prestige, begin to settle into a comfort zone that takes their focus off what got them there. They close their eyes to all of their personal trials, believing that their corporate struggles deserve more attention. Eventually, their success begins to unravel because they violated the principle of 'first things first' by not placing issues on the home front before workplace matters. Over time, personal defeats begin to overshadow any corporate success they may have had.

A comfort zone is that 'feel good' mental place we carve out of our existence that we can retreat to in times of difficulty. Because this place offers so much comfort and apparent safety, most people allow their islands of comfort to keep them from stretching beyond the limits of those havens. Because comfort zones offer us serene retirement from the challenges of daily life, we must resist the temptation to spend every waking moment there…and get on with the business of working toward fulfilling our dreams. You will always know the extent to which you will make great sacrifice to secure your success because your comfort zone has already staked out that proverbial line in the sand—beyond which you will not venture. If you are not careful, your comfort zone will not only dictate what you will do to obtain your goals, but it will also determine what blessings never make their way into your life, as well. Do not allow a comfort zone to deny you your due reward, and never build a monument to your accomplishments when victory is still at bay.

Weakness Exposes Strength

One of the greatest strengths that a person can display is the admission of certain vulnerability. Your susceptibility is not your prison but rather your freedom. Knowing where you are weak allows you to know how and where to fill the breach in your defenses. No one on the face of this Earth exists without weaknesses. That is why no man is an island; we all need each other. Pinpointing your weaknesses is crucial to your being able to focus on honing your strengths. In war, the pincer movement or double envelopment (as it is commonly called) is a basic military strategy that is only successful to the extent that the enemy believes he has found a weakness in the opposing lines. Once he is drawn into the center of the line, the opposing force can then envelop him on both sides with overwhelming strength of numbers.

> No one on the face of this Earth exists without weaknesses.

So, there are times when knowing your weaknesses can be used to your advantage. Trying to conquer Goliath is foolish if you are unaware of your vulnerabilities. It is impossible to be strong everywhere at all times. If you try, you will spread yourself too thin and render yourself defenseless. History has clearly proved in both sport and war that an over-confident opponent tends to step onto the field of strife without the proper training because he believes he is about to face an inferior opponent. Your apparent weaknesses will cause your opponent to relax the standards of his usual regimen, which offers you an opportunity to exploit such cockiness, whether in war or in business.

Be Careful and Pay Attention

Be careful to whom you pay attention when you are in the midst of personal battles. The people who pretend to have all the answers for your situation oftentimes have no history of accomplishments to substantiate their role as your counselor. The advice they give is often a cover to mask their own deficiencies. Just because you may be experiencing difficulties in your life, doesn't mean you are doing something wrong. On the contrary, you are more than likely doing something right. Troubles sometimes show up just because you are doing the right thing.

Therefore, rise to the occasion and allow the champion in you to come forth.

The Rule of First Things First

WE CAN FORM NO HABIT without our actions first coming under the influence of the principle of "first things." The law of first things is very simple. It means that the initial time something is produced, done, spoken or even thought leaves its stamp on all subsequent occurrences to mirror it. In order words, it sets precedents for everything from its kind.

The first time you attempt to do any new task, you will find that it is difficult and awkward to perform. However, the more you work through the mechanics of that task, the easier it becomes. Therefore, when learning anything new, focus on mastering fundamental techniques. Place all of your emphasis on what you do first, so that you will reap a harvest of intended results.

Addicts—whether hooked on drugs, alcohol, or cigarettes—are not born; they are made. People do not come into the world bound to certain substances. Constant use produces addictive behavior. When we introduce chemicals or substances into our bodies, regardless of what

> Constant use produces addictive behavior.

they are, the foreign matter will inevitably alter the way our bodies work. Over time, the substances change the entire nature of the host body. Before you know it, you become a slave to the very thing you were designed to master. In other words, cigarettes cause a smoker's body to undergo certain physiological changes in order to adapt to new conditions, which often lead to cancer.

You will become a slave to every choice—good or bad—you make in life. There is no escaping that fact. Therefore, carefully consider your choices before making them. Every millionaire I have ever encountered shared the exact same fact. They all said that it is much easier to make subsequent millions than the first. Learn to do things right the first time and subsequent attempts will be a 'piece of cake.' Once you master the fundamentals of success in any area, you will then attract the materials of that success. Vince Lombardi once said, "Winning is a habit. Unfortunately, so is losing."

If there is a formula for success, there must be a recipe for disaster. Both will only occur after 'first things' are established. Success in life—whether in business, marriage, finances, etc.—begins with the kind of information you are programmed to follow. The human mind is the most sophisticated and powerful computer ever conceived, but its potential is wasted if no information or the wrong type of information gets embedded into it. Your mind can serve you well, and it can fail you miserably—based on YOUR programming. The information flowing around in your mind makes all the difference when it comes to determining the size of the world in which you choose to live. Your mind is the hard drive that stores the data, which connects you to all you will ever need or desire in life. The problem is that so many other people have been tapping its potential, except you.

> *"I think the principle of 'first things first' does apply, and has to be followed if we are to have any chance of success."*
> —Al Gore

The Rule of First Things First

Your thinking is always the place to begin to implement effective and lasting change. When you believe strongly that you can succeed, you usually do. When you doubt your abilities, failure is much more likely the result. I believe also that confidence, focus, and practice all factor into the formula for success in life. You possess the power and ability to radically improve your life. You will reap quality from your life experiences if you first place quality in all you do.

> When you doubt your abilities, failure is much more likely the result.

Back from Divorce

I TITLED THIS CHAPTER SIMPLY *Back from Divorce* because when I experienced one of my own, it seemed as though I had gotten 'Lost in Space'. During that painful episode in my life, I went through my daily routines perfunctorily, all the while pondering how this could have happened to me. Without realizing it, I had slipped into a state of functional depression. This was a tremendous blow to my ego because I had always considered myself to be very levelheaded and always certain of my bearings in life. Suddenly, I was not certain of anything.

My entire world was turned upside down. My personal income took an immediate nosedive; my housing arrangement became tenuous; and my relationship with my three children became strained beyond belief. I thought my life was over and done with. What hurt the most was how

> Divorce rips asunder the very foundation of a family and sends its members spiraling downhill into great emotional upheaval.

the divorce affected my kids. I never wanted them to ever be deprived of my fatherly influence in their lives, and for the first time, they were. I prayed fervently that God would help me to one day regain my rightful role in their lives, as well as in their hearts. Because of my profound love for them, I couldn't bear not seeing and interacting with them on a daily basis.

You see, I grew up without my biological father's influence in my life. I had vowed to myself early on that I would always be there for my children, whenever I had kids of my own. Yet, my divorce caused me to breech the very oath I had sworn to uphold. In my estimation, divorce has to rank as the most devastating catastrophe a family can ever experience because in the midst of it, everyone suffers considerable loss. Divorce rips asunder the very foundation of a family and sends its members spiraling downhill into great emotional upheaval. It is no small wonder why divorce is like the ripping apart of the flesh that joins two people. The Bible is very explicit when it declares, "What God has joined together let no man put asunder."

The pain of my divorce caused me to be anesthetized to everything else around me. I thought I would never be able to rebound from that major setback…until one day, while sitting alone in my house with one worn couch and a bed, I heard the doorbell. I wondered who could be ringing my doorbell. When I opened the door, my heart lifted when I saw Elder Fred Crawford standing there. He was like a father to me, and I had always considered him to be one of my greatest mentors. Although I was very happy to see him, I was so embarrassed about the divorce that I could hardly hold my head up.

As we sat on one of only two pieces of furniture in the entire place, we discussed my situation. Elder Crawford said something to me that I will never forget as long as I live—something I bring to the forefront of my thoughts whenever I experience the kind of trials that bring out the skeptics and naysayers. He simply said, "Get up and stop giving these people something to talk about!" I am certain he said more than that, but these profound words are the only ones I can recall from his visit. His unexpected visitation and heart-lifting words were enough to bring me back from the brink of despair to walk once again among the living. For the first time in a long time, I saw a reason to go on living.

The moment I decided to stop dying from the wound caused by my divorce is the moment I started living again. Nowadays, I live with the sober understanding that my past may be tainted, but my future is indeed spotless. That day with Elder Crawford, my hope was renewed and my mental perspective concerning my divorce changed immediately. It all started to change as soon as I stopped thinking like a victim and started thinking like a victor. I will not pretend that everything around me changed quickly or overnight; that certainly was not the case. However, everything within my heart and mind changed the very instant I heard and accepted Elder Crawford's dictate to me. My emotional state was no longer unstable; I had regained my footing. Over time, my situation began to correspond to the positive change that occurred within me.

It has been twenty years since my divorce. According to the relationship I now have with my children, my influence in their lives has been fully restored...and then some.

Divorce not only devastates families, but it also injures relatives, friends, and business dealings. Although I do not advocate divorce, I do encourage anyone who has ever experienced its painful legacy to continue living after the marriage has ended. There is life after a divorce. If you have ever experienced divorce or are presently embroiled in its ugly proceedings, allow me to help you stop the bleeding. Do not let your mistakes or misfortunes rob you of your fortune!

Pardon me Sir, but...YOUR LIFE is calling. So, let's put some pep in that step!

> There is life after a divorce.

A Simple Solution for Simple Problems

HERE IS A REMEDY FOR BEING cantankerous and just plain irritated with life. Instead of pretending to be cheerful about the circumstances that seem to be getting the best of you, take a pragmatic approach to fixing the whole matter.

I discovered long ago that circumstances, by themselves, do not create the moods we feel; people create the atmosphere for what they feel. Your mind is in no way preconditioned to respond to a given set of circumstances—ones that cause the needle to respond erratically on your emotional Richter scale.

People have simply learned over time to associate emotional responses with certain occurrences. In essence, our emotional states are accustomed to dwelling alongside certain outside stimuli or situations. Based upon certain events we experience in life, our emotional responses get inextricably linked to those events. This stimulus-emotion association process takes years to cement in our minds; therefore, it will require concerted effort on your part to break the vicious cycle of falling

> Complaining about your circumstances will not fix them.

into certain emotional ruts based on the circumstances that surround you. It is not easy to embrace joy and dawn a smile when your financial life is in disarray.

I would like to recommend a very simple and practical answer to the depressing mood swings that keep you in your emotional doldrums. The solution will not take nearly as long as it took you to learn your counterproductive stimulus-emotional habits. You need not be a rocket scientist or a mathematician to apply this technique. All you need to know is how to add. Are you ready to discover how to escape being an emotional slave to your circumstances?

The solution is this...you must learn to count your blessings or they do not count! "What?" you may be asking yourself. I know that you thought that the remedy would involve a more complicated process. On the contrary, simple solutions will often address our most pressing problems.

Count your blessings. Take inventory of all the wonderful relationships, talents, abilities, and resources you currently have at your disposal. If you would do this, I am certain you would conclude that you have much for which to be thankful. When you compare your present condition to a much worse one, you will see things from a more sober perspective. Oftentimes, people only consider the negatives in a sea full of positives. There are more things working in your favor than are working against you. When you begin to count your blessings, you will notice how the good will far outweigh your bad. Therefore, begin by thanking God!

Complaining about your circumstances will not fix them; it will only exacerbate your situation. However, if you count the good things that can come out of a bad situation, you will cause your emotional responses to react favorably instead of negatively. Try it; it works.

Overcoming Opposition

I HAVE BEEN IN MANY PERSONAL BATTLES in my lifetime. From every skirmish won or lost, I walked away from each incident having gained valuable insights and perspectives on life. I believe that life is a series of lessons and tests. The many struggles and adversities that we will encounter throughout our lives must serve as gauges to indicate our level of progress. Trials surface in our lives to reveal weaknesses—those areas where some sort of attention and fortification are necessary. Opposition may also reveal strengths, but this is usually not their prescribed purpose.

> Do not assume that a "one size fits all" approach to dealing with difficulty in your life will suffice.

Regardless of how and why they enter our lives, keep in mind one thing regarding your struggles. Every opposition you encounter must be tackled with a different strategy, from an entirely different perspective. Do not assume that a "one size fits all" approach to dealing with difficulty in your life will suffice. What may have worked in one situation may not be sufficient to slay the dragon in the next, even if the circumstances bear an uncanny resemblance to each other.

Why is this so? Consider for a moment what happens when you perform the same workout routine day in and day out for an extended period time, without any variation in your program. Before long, your muscles will begin to adjust to the routine, and you will experience the law of diminishing returns. Your muscles, although taxed by the workout, no longer reap results because they have gotten used to your routine. In other words, your muscles have figured you out and are one step ahead of you in your training. Therefore, despite the pressure and tribulation you attempt to exert on your muscles to produce growth, they are unable to respond because the challenges are always the same. In order to grow, they must be hit from different angles and from various different perspectives. Fitness experts label this approach "muscle confusion training." The goal is keep the muscles in a constant state of confusion so they never have an opportunity to fall into a routine, thereby allowing you to achieve maximum fitness results.

I used that analogy to paint a picture. You are the muscles that need to be exercised in order to experience personal growth. The obstacles and challenges you encounter in life are the fitness experts that come on the scene in order to work you out. These fitness trainers, however, will not afford you the luxury of falling into a dull routine. They will keep you off balance by constantly varying the workout plan. Therefore, you must make constant adjustments if you are to keep pace. If you attempt to resist their workout plan by applying the same old effort, you may get swept downstream.

The trials you face are so surgical in their attack that they hone in on all your weaknesses, which are constantly changing as you mature. What may have easily unsettled your world as a young teen may not even register on your emotional Richter scale as an adult. Then again, as you journey through life, the complexity of the problems you face tends to escalate as well. As a result, you are constantly gathering new weaknesses as you grow and develop as a person. So, do not assume that you can carry forward the momentum from previous victory onto the battlefield of your present confrontation.

Some people respond poorly under pressure while others thrive in the face of it. Regardless of how you stack up under the weight of pressure, remember that how you fare in the end—when all is said and done—is the only thing that determines success or failure.

Victory in life does not come without a price tag. Sometimes that price tag is in the form of blood and tears. At other times, your victory may demand precious blood, sweat and tears…and everything in between. If you ever expect to achieve any measure of success—whether in your marriage, your business life, your financial affairs, or your spiritual life—understand that you will encounter many battles. Do not shy away from these crucial tests, because after you successfully pass them, only then will you have a testimony from which others will draw strength.

The Secret to Perseverance

NOT LONG AGO, my wife and I had the privilege of meeting Sylvia Woods, widely regarded as the "Queen of Soulfood." She is the owner of Sylvia's Restaurant in the historical village of Harlem. She is also a best-selling cookbook author. Her journey to carve out a place in history is a tale of inspiration and encouragement for anyone who has ever thought of fulfilling a dream.

At the time of our meeting, Mrs. Woods was 82 years old. To this day, she continues to manage her businesses with her adult children, albeit on a part-time basis nowadays. Still very lucid in her thoughts, she never shies away from recounting the story of her humble start and the challenges attendant to her rise to worldwide notoriety. Her once humble kitchen diner now encompasses an entire city block in Harlem, New York where her famous restaurant now stands.

> Challenges are embedded in your journey of becoming great, and they can never be sidestepped, erased or aborted.

Unexpected Treasures

In our conversation, Mrs. Woods discussed how she grew to become the owner of a business enterprise that consists of Sylvia's Restaurant, Sylvia's Catering Corp., a nationwide line of Sylvia's Food Products, several bestselling cookbooks, and a real estate firm. She boldly proclaims that God is the sole reason for her success. Additionally, she gives God all the credit for every door He opened for her, openly admitting that her journey was not an easy one.

In fact, she continued to reiterate how difficult it was in the beginning, operating a black-owned restaurant in a drug- and gang-infested area during the 60s. "Drug addicts were so prevalent that I just decided to feed them and they never gave me any problems," said Mrs. Woods.

From her story and from countless other such testimonials, it is clear to see that great success comes only after great struggle is waged and is overcome. On the other hand, goals that are easily achieved will not produce the requisite perseverance conducive to winning life's battles.

While Sylvia Woods is quick to point out that God is the one who opened every door to her success, she is just as quick to highlight the fact that tribulation was just as much a part of getting her to the top. So, even though God may open the door for you, you will have to endure trials, tribulations, and struggles in order to taste victory. They are embedded in your journey to becoming great, and they can never be sidestepped, erased or aborted.

I have learned that the bigger the challenge (giant), the greater the reward! If it were easy, then everyone would accomplish his or her dreams in life. When your peers surrender to the demands of tough times, you must move beyond your struggles in order to claim victory.

Through perseverance, you will gain the necessary knowledge to combat and conquer your fears and overcome your challenges. Life experiences assume greater significance, notwithstanding all the challenges or stresses, when you are able to taste of the victory of your hard-fought battles.

Therefore, never give up while in pursuit of your dreams, because perseverance will qualify you for the victory at journey's end.

Divorce Statistics and What They Mean to You

THE MAJORITY OF REASONS PUT FORTH to explain the contributing causes of divorce are simply byproducts of much deeper personal defects. With most marriages, partners tend to fixate on trivial matters and give little attention to issues that matter most.

Americans know all too well that the survival rate in this country for marriage runs around 50 percent. More troubling is the fact that the failure rate of those who marry the second time is somewhere between 60–67 percent; and third time marriages fail a rate of 73–74 percent.

These divorce statistics should suggest that there are many reasons why marriages fail. Divorced individuals cite lack of communication or poor communication as the number one reason for their dissolved unions—how strange that happily married couples contribute their marital bliss to healthy communication.

> Divorce statistics mean absolutely nothing to you when divorce is not an option.

I do not claim to know everything there is to know about marriage. As a certified marriage counselor with more than twenty-five years of Family Life counseling experience, however, I have seen enough of what does and does not work in marriage. In my book, *How to Fix Your Marriage without Using a Hammer,* I pour out my many years of observations on this particular topic. I have gotten in the trenches with couples more times over the past twenty-five years than I can remember. I have been there to help guide them out of turbulent waters and see them come to rest on solid foundations.

In my book as well as in my counseling sessions, I tend to focus more on solutions than on problems. I figure it this way, spending time laying a proper foundation ensures that a bad one never takes hold. It is, therefore, more profitable and time-efficient to build one's house on a solid rock than on shifting sand.

Individuals must be honest with themselves and with their spouses. When you commit to working on your faults—not your spouse's—you will notice how quickly problems begin to disappear. This undertaking will prove difficult, as our first inclination is to point the finger away from ourselves. We, by nature, are not inclined to step up to the plate when problems come knocking. Our first instinct is to send a surrogate. If, however, each person in a marriage relationship would go through moments of introspection, individuals would then place themselves on the altar of sacrifice rather than the other person.

Marriage can work if you learn to apply the proper principles. When you do, you will discover the joy of marriage, rather than experiencing its unintended pitfalls.

Seven Steps to Enjoy Your Life

IS LIFE MOVING SO FAST that you find it difficult to keep pace? On the other hand, is life so ho-hum that every day seems just like the one before it, leaving you unable to recognize where one ends and a new one begins?

Many people have lost their zest for life. This gloomy outlook usually stems from severe disappointment with where a person's life has taken him or her. Consequently, many individuals incorrectly conclude that it is too late to chase their dreams.

Perhaps you may feel as though your mistakes in life are too disastrous for recovery to be possible. Such despondency has a tendency to spill over into every area of a person's life, if it is not addressed. It will affect your marriage, your work, and the raising of your children.

> Life is brief, just like this chapter.

If you live your days with unfulfilled aspirations, chances are you will soon retreat into a state of depression. From there, you will assume a victim's mentality and take on a defeated attitude.

Unexpected Treasures

There are steps you can take to prevent this downhill spiral and ensure that you improve the condition of your journey through life.

1. Depend on God for direction and strength (willpower is no match for life's great trials)
2. Understand Purpose (purpose adds meaning to our lives)
3. Become Highly Selective (right words spoken can lubricate life's frictions)
4. Control Your Mind (if you can control your thoughts, you can direct your life)
5. Don't Sweat It (major on the primary, not on the inconsequential)
6. Enjoy Life (life is an investment, not a waste)
7. Repeat Step One (start and end each day with trusting God)

Must I follow the steps in the order listed to be effective? No, not at all! Endeavor to begin and end with steps one and seven, as God is crucial to the success of all our pursuits. However, you can perform steps two through six in any order you choose.

Who is Cheating You?

I RECENTLY ASKED A SERIES OF QUESTIONS to a group of people to get at the issue of self-imposed limitations. I simply wanted the individuals to identify how their limitations were determined. Oftentimes, people play themselves cheap because of the bad information they have taken in over the years—information that we gather from significant others, such as teachers, parents, friends, co-workers, or spouses. Because of the influential role they played in our lives, we tend to carry around with us for a long time their words of positivity or negativity. For some strange reason, their negative words tend to outweigh the effect of positives words, for most people. Why then is it that...

> You have no more and no less than what you believe you are entitled to receive.

When anyone comes along and tries to speak into us words that are uplifting, creative, and powerful, our first tendency is to shun those words because they often run counter to our belief systems. The type of information you take in on a consistent basis will determine what you believe you can either accomplish or have in life.

Be careful what you allow your mind to receive, because the information will become mental photographs that will show you either opportunities or limitations.

What would be your response if a very wealthy person handed you a credit card and gave you the green light to purchase whatever your heart desired? Let us be honest! Would you buy what you really wanted or would you impose a spending cap on your desires, ensuring that your purchase aligns with what you feel you are entitled to enjoy? Ninety-nine percent of people asked this question said they would probably not buy what they really desired.

Our excuses for being frugal would probably be, "I was not informed as to the credit card limit," or "You never told me what I could buy." The truth of the matter is the individuals knew fully the conditions of the offer. The wealthy individual clearly stipulated the parameters of their spending in the offer.

The problem is that the beneficiaries of this generous offer did not believe fully in what they had heard. The 99 percent of individuals receiving the credit card offer, therefore, set their own limit without any assistance and thus purchased items based on their standard alone.

Somehow, we will find ways to shift our self-imposed limitations onto those who may hold the key to our blessings, as this credit card illustration depicts. However, despite how you may personally feel about your life, you have no more and no less than what you believe you are entitled to receive. Therefore, change what you believe, and the size of your world will change in direct proportion to your level of belief.

Stop cheating yourself out of life's riches!

The Dream Provides the Means

THE MOST WIDELY-USED VEHICLE in human history was the Model T. First introduced in 1908, it had total sales revenue of $10,607 that first year. Within four years, however, annual sales had jumped to $168,304, and in four more years, they had reached $730,041. In 1919, Henry Ford bought out the minority stockholders for nearly $106 million. They had an initial investment of only $33,100—what an astronomical return on investment!

During the Model T's lifetime (1908–1927), production totaled 15,458,781 cars—more than the combined total for all other cars for those years.

57 Varieties is one business endeavor that did not follow the path of others. When the will of Henry J. Heinz—wealthy distributor of the famous "57 Varieties" line—was read, it was found to contain the following confession:

> God does not determine how much a person will have in this life—each decides for him or herself.

Unexpected Treasures

"Looking forward to the time when my earthly career will end, I desire to set forth at the very beginning of this will, as the most important item in it, a confession of my faith in Jesus Christ as my Savior. I also desire to bear witness to the fact that throughout my life, in which there were unusual joys and sorrows, I have been wonderfully sustained by my faith in God through Jesus Christ. This legacy was left me by my consecrated mother, a woman of strong faith, and to it I attribute any success I have attained."

Success is living the life God intended for you. I strongly believe that God gives humankind the capacity to create wealth, but God is not the determining factor of how much of it we are to have. Each individual is completely responsible for living his or her own dream. God provides the dream; when lived, the dream provides the means.

Henry Ford and Henry Heinz made extraordinary achievements and were able to help thousands through their philanthropic giving. If you want to be a blessing to others, live the dream God gave you, and you will have treasures beyond riches.

Want More, Learn More

IF YOU WANT TO EARN MORE, you have to learn more. What do you do when your existing plan continues to fall short of producing any desired increase? What would you do if someone presented you with a new plan that would guarantee reduced stress while maximizing a return on the talents you already possess?

Everyone needs to learn when to abort a bad game plan and how to adopt a winning strategy—which is the most effective way to change your results. The primary ingredients of greatness are unwavering faith mixed with a solid plan for achieving success. Every person needs a plan in order to succeed.

> Everyone needs to learn when to abort a bad game plan and how to adopt a winning strategy.

The amount of detail you incorporate into your strategy determines the ease with which you are able to navigate clearly from one point to the next. However, a plan without the requisite faith to execute it means nothing. Faith is crucial to any plan you develop because it allows you to see the desired end-state before you get there.

As you journey along the path of your plan, do not forget the power of prayer. Prayer allows you to access God's inexhaustible power in order to accomplish what is humanly impossible. In the Bible, Jesus exhorts His disciples, when they pray, to believe that they have already received whatever they requested in prayer. In effect, He told them to act as though they had already received the physical manifestation of their desires the moment they prayed. It is important to understand that true faith accepts the matter to be a done deal; even though the physical object of your faith may not have materialized yet.

What happens if there is a conflict between my conscious and subconscious minds? While it may be easier to reprogram my subconscious, what do I do if my conscious mind refuses to accept the idea of my becoming a wealthy success? The key to solving this dilemma is repetition, which, after all, is the mother of all learning. You must continue to say to yourself, "I know I can! I know I can!" until you imbed the reality of your words deep within the fiber of your being. Moreover, you must first recognize that you can achieve everything that you can dare to believe, based upon God's Word.

Some years ago, I woke up to the reality that God does not dictate how much wealth we accumulate. He left that for each individual to decide. Every person has the ability to create wealth. What you learn about wealth and how you choose to respect it, determines how much of it you will earn. Learn more about how money functions in a free market economy and how wealth is actually established; then you will watch your money work to make you wealthy.

How to Fine-Tune Your Mentality

WHAT KIND OF MENTALITY would you say you have? Do you have the kind that is prone to quitting or succeeding? Do you think more like a poor victim or a wealthy achiever? Do you offer excuses for underachieving or do you accept responsibility for your failings in life?

Perhaps these questions are a bit tough to process, but I intentionally came out of the starting gate with these penetrating questions to cause you to think about your mental make-up.

I know that introspection is never an easy exercise to undertake, without walking away overly critical of what one may discover. I assure you that my intent is not to impair your psyche. Instead, I desire to strengthen it. If you continue to read these powerful attitude adjustors, you will reap an abundant crop of wisdom that will make your journey through life much easier.

> What you spend the largest percentage of your time doing can often point to what you love.

How does one move from having a mindset of scarcity to one of abundance?

In my book *Beyond Ordinary,* I state that the most difficult thing to change is you. Changing your mentality in order to accomplish a goal or to improve one's marriage or increase your income is not an easy undertaking. People have undergone hypnosis, counseled with motivational gurus, and even tried religious meditation. These attempts to change, while sincere, rarely produce any noticeable or lasting benefits.

How did you arrive at your present mentality? While it may seem like a difficult task to determine where you developed your mental framework, the clues may be right under your nose. What kind of people do you spend most of your time with and what is the nature of their conversation? What do you watch on television or listen to on the radio every day? You are a product of your environment. You are what you consume daily. Therefore, the key to true change is a change of environment, which you have the power to orchestrate.

What you spend the largest percentage of your time doing can often point to what you love. Have you ever heard the phrase, "You are what you eat?" Well, it is true. It is also true that you are a product of the information you take in daily, from whatever source. YOU ARE A PRODUCT OF YOUR INFORMATION! Change your information source and you will change your life.

Researchers have observed that your income is an average of the income of your ten closest friends. You may be surprised at how easily your life can improve by simply reshuffling some of your friends from the bottom to the top. Iron does sharpen iron!

A Premier Life Principle

I HAVE BOTH LEARNED AND TAUGHT many success principles during my journey in life, but one truth stands out among them all. It is far more difficult to finish something than to start it. This may be the premier reason why there are so many great starters but few great finishers.

The reason that there are so many great starters and so few great finishers is that it typically takes much less effort to start anything than it does to see it through to its completion. Therefore, when the start goes according to plan, individuals get lulled into a false sense of

> When you exercise perseverance, you will always outlast your challenges.

what the balance of the journey is going to be like. Doubts begin to set in, however, when the snowball begins to grow and momentum begins to slow. Just when the snowball begins to roll back down the hill, more effort and tenacity are required to continue the uphill climb. At this point, most people simply quit.

Unexpected Treasures

Most people conclude erroneously that the trials that accompany success are there to impede progress forever.

The law of Starting and Finishing is an actual principle, just as valid as the law of Sowing and Reaping. Both principles govern success in any arena, whether with respect to a person or a thing. The law of Starting and Finishing suggests that the closer you get to the completion of anything, the more you deplete your natural abilities. Therefore, in order for a person to complete a particular project, he must learn to draw on inner strength in order to finish the task, as natural abilities begin to wane.

In 1998, my church, under my supervision, started construction on a brand new 42,000 square foot church facility. With an entire congregation behind me, our initial push allowed us to complete only 26,000 square feet of the overall structure. At times, I must admit, it seemed that we would never be able to complete what we had started. Despite the many challenges I endured for nine full years, however, I never stopped believing that we would one day be able to utilize the entire facility.

Well…after nine grueling years of constant struggle and rising construction costs, our worship facility is finally 100 percent completed. The level of difficulty you will experience during the home stretch of your endeavors is the reason so many people fail to reach the end of their struggles to enjoy their dreams. With our construction project, I personally resolved that regardless of how long the process took, I would see it through to completion.

When you exercise perseverance, you will always outlast your challenges. Life does not penalize you for how long it takes to achieve your goals. It does not matter when you finish; it matters that you finish.

Don't Drop Your Day Job to Begin Living Your Dreams

THIS CHAPTER MAY BE A DIFFICULT ONE to follow, but before you dismiss what I share here, read it in its entirety.

In general, people fail to understand just how working a job is actually exercising their ability to create wealth. One reason for this is that they tend to dislike the job they have.

If you see your job merely as an occupation, then that is all it will ever do—simply occupy your time. However, if you regard your job as a vocation, then you will find that it is more fulfilling, because somehow you are able to attach purpose and a higher calling to what you do. You will never find fulfillment in a job that fails to serve a purpose higher than simply earning money.

> The most difficult image to change is the one you have of yourself.

What is the difference between what a prostitute does for a living and what you do to earn money? Not one single thing! You both are doing what you feel you need to do in order to survive. Neither of you may like your chosen profession, but, like her, you may feel powerless to change how you make money.

The most difficult image to change is the one you have of yourself. When it comes to self-esteem, people generally are unhappy with the person they see in the mirror each day. As a result, they allow feelings of low self-esteem to translate into a lack of self-confidence. Because of our natural inclinations, we are more likely to listen to the voice of our past failures and disappointments rather than to the voice of our dreams that beckons us from our future.

Despite what you may do to earn money, you must in every instance exercise your God-given talents to do so. Therefore, you should ensure that you focus your efforts on areas of life where you are able to maximize the return on your investment of talent and energy. A good place to start is with the things you like to do. You do not have to quit your job right away to begin living your dreams. Ease into it and make a full commitment to the pursuit of your dream only when you are in a financial position to do so.

Unless your dream can produce more income from the start than your current job, I recommend that you hold onto that job. You will know when it is the right time to leave your nine-to-five job. I would encourage you, though, to trust in God, and seek His direction in all of your pursuits. He will direct you to that place of perfect peace and contentment.

Believe What You Know

HAVE YOU EVER THOUGHT ABOUT the large volume of information you have stored in your mind? Your brain is the most sophisticated computing device on the planet. It is vast enough to store all the data you have taken in since your birth—from all the five sensory input sources. What you do not currently know, your brain can gather, without losing the capacity to acquire more information. Our minds never experience a hard drive overload. The potential we have between two ears is simply astounding. What amazes me, though, is the number of people who second-guess their own potential. They can know something thoroughly and later doubt what they have placed upstairs. They simply do not trust their great capacity to absorb information, convert it to knowledge and recall it at will.

> Your mind is not as limited as you may believe, but computers are.

Insecurity is common among people who are accustomed to living their lives in the bed of uncertainty. To understand the potential of the human mind, you need only examine a complex computer, since computers are simply downgraded versions of the brain—whether human or animal. The human brain does not act like a computer; the last time I checked, the brain was around a lot longer than computer technology. Therefore, computers mimic the intricacies of the brain. They take in data; they process that data; and they spit out calculations. But...

It helps to understand the power of that computing device you have upstairs by explaining things in the reverse order. Therefore, it is much easier to facilitate discussion by suggesting that our minds work like computers, since we can see, touch and handle them (computers that is).

Like computers, we need to have data fed into our systems in order for us to function—that is to think, act, react, feel, and grow. However, your mind is not limited, but computers are.

Man can think, reason, and figure out complex problems that have nothing to do with numerical calculation. Furthermore, he can perform everything God created him to do. Man invented computers and all of their capabilities. Just who do you think wrote the voluminous encyclopedias and dictionaries you go to for yet more information? And... Who came up with Google?

Humans have fashioned great architectural wonders for millennia. Engineers have calculated weights, loads, capacities, heights, and distances for erecting great monuments long before computers and calculators ever entered the mind of man. Contrary to popular belief, you can do anything you think and believe you can do. Use your mind to think and imagine, but use your heart to believe in your God-given capabilities. Stop waiting for absolute certainty before starting a business or venturing toward greatness.

An old beer commercial used to claim, "You only go around once in life, so you have to reach for all the gusto you can." I have modified and adopted that phrase to mean (for me) that from now on, I am going to be a gusto grabber.

Go for the gold in all you do!

Essentials for Reaching the Top: Principles for Staying There

It takes a lot of effort to reach the top, but it requires even more to stay there. It is disgraceful when a person gains so much through hard work but loses it all through willful negligence or mismanagement. If experience teaches anything, it is that the majority of us do not learn from it. In general, people willfully travel down the same road that consistently dooms its victims to failure, with little regard for the consequences. When this happens, people tend to blame others for their misfortunes.

> Learn as you grow; but...earn as you learn.

No Shortcuts

There are countless ways to invest money. However, there is but one option available when it comes to fulfilling your dreams. The New Year always begins with great promises but ends with breached commitments, and somewhere in between, people tend to defer or dash the vows they pledge to themselves. Each year you repeat this cycle, your fervor to chase your dream diminishes by bits and pieces. Instead of gaining momentum, your climb just gets steeper. Endeavor to make substantive progress toward your goals every year.

Fulfilling Your Goals

The big picture is important, but not as important as the smaller puzzle pieces that make up the whole. You must view every experience as an integral piece of your destiny. Failure is just as important as success. Setbacks cultivate perseverance and tenacity, while your critics should serve as stepping stones to higher levels. Remember, Rome was not built in a day; neither are dreams!

Staying on Top

The trials of your journey are essential for your survival once you arrive at your destination. Do not faint under their weight; they are merely pieces of a much bigger puzzle. If anything, allow their growing nature and intensity to indicate how close to the prize you actually are. Your troubles can teach you a great deal—namely when to move from your present place of contentment. Therefore, learn as you grow, but… earn as you learn.

My Final Advice

My final advice to you is this… Value every personal connection you establish; be creative with every situation handed to you; and challenge yourself to stretch beyond all self-imposed limitations. There is so much to learn from your daily experiences. If you are observant, you will realize that your experiences are simply snapshots that expose to you thousands of new ways to exploit opportunity.

Remember, you can be anything in the world you want to be. Above all, be YOU!

What Motivates You?

WHAT DOES IT TAKE TO GET YOU pumped and energized concerning the fulfillment of your goals and aspirations? The answer to this question can vary from person to person. However, there is one thing that remains constant for everyone. You need a catalyst to get the wheels turning; otherwise, starting any venture becomes a difficult proposition for anyone.

Some people allow fear to hinder them from starting and pressing forward while others move beyond their fears

> Many prizefighters will sacrifice nearly everything to escape painful backgrounds.

in order to undertake particular endeavors. Completing a thing is an entirely different story; but one thing is certain, you cannot finish what you never start.

There is an Art to every Start. While this may sound cliché, it is true, nevertheless.

In order to pursue your objectives and goals in life, you need some form of motivation or motive to move. The word "motivation" derives from the words "move" and "cause or reason." Thus, motivation is simply the impetus that causes a particular thing to move. What is the passionate driving force in your life—the thing that pushes you more than any other thing?

For some people, making a lot of money is motivation enough to get them headed in a certain direction. Helping others drives compassionate individuals to do what they do, while invention and discovery puts the gears in motion for the entrepreneurial types. For game hunters, the thrill of the hunt is sufficient motive for them to travel halfway around the world to bag one trophy to hang over the fireplace.

Despite how lofty or modest your ambitions may be, you need ample motivation of some sort to pursue them. Even then, your motivation will demand a reason for being, before you can even begin to assert one single desire. Professional boxers oftentimes use poverty or the dangerous neighborhood conditions of their pasts to motivate them to reach for the prize that goes along with being the champion. Many prizefighters will sacrifice nearly everything to escape painful backgrounds. Fleeing the past, therefore, becomes motivation enough to endure grueling training and unimaginable dangers in the ring. Such tales have become the inspiration for many great feature-length movies like "Rocky" and "Cinderella Man."

Some things in life will never call upon all of your passion and energies in order to pursue them. The truth is…not everything in life deserves that much of us. The things that do, however, should receive all of you. To be able to give your very best at the start of every round you encounter in life, you must identify the cause or the reason for your motivation. Otherwise, victory will remain elusive. On the other hand…

Identify your motivation to answer the call of the destiny that will take you to center ring. Once you identify the significance of what you are fighting for, victory can be yours.

56 Real Teamwork

Teamwork is a word conveniently thrown around by those who stand on the sidelines while others actually do all the heavy lifting. These Monday night quarterbacks have all the advice, but no record of accomplishments to suggest that they took any risks in life.

Those individuals who scream the loudest about how others need to come together as a team are often the first ones to declare their unwillingness to become part of the solution by joining a team effort. They blame their lack of commitment on their not wanting to side with a weak team or a doomed venture. They will never join in until they can eliminate every possible chance of failure, by stacking their team with only heavy-hitters. In effect, they are simply trying to hide their shortcomings by surrounding themselves with proven producers. Consequently, they compromise overall team strength by their internal character weaknesses, which eventually become apparent.

> Team effectiveness is certain when every team member works to achieve the same common goals.

Critics rarely understand what it takes to become true team players. They stand on the sidelines and loudly proclaim to others what they need to do. Yet, they are never willing to assume the responsibility of risk, for fear that others might discover their ineptitude and sheer folly.

With any undertaking, followers are just as important as leaders. It is important, however, for leaders to ensure that their followers understand clearly and adhere fully to the leader's instructions, or else chaos will ensue. Team effectiveness is certain when every team member works to achieve the same common goals.

No team can achieve success without a good leader, but no leader can ever lead effectively without loyal and faithful followers. Individual team members should strive to become effective followers before seeking positions of leadership. Good followers make good leaders. Great followers have gone on to become great leaders themselves. On the other hand, rotten followers invariably turn out to become dangerous and stubborn leaders.

Before closing this segment, I would like to discuss briefly the silent follower—the type of individual who can be dangerous to the overall morale of any team. They seek only to do their job without looking to help the team in general, or helping others do their jobs better. They do not try to build camaraderie or help to instill confidence in teammates. Additionally, they seldom have an opinion and are oftentimes vague when asked questions.

Good followers do not seek to do their jobs only, but they identify ways to aid others to improve their performance as well. They understand that individual success does not necessarily translate to team success. Individual success—while others may applaud it—is rarely respected. We tend to remember fondly individuals who sacrifice individual ambitions for the sake of overall team victory. Twelve disciples subordinated their personal agendas so that Jesus could fulfill His purpose on Earth. Today, we are the beneficiaries of their selfless acts.

Reaching Your Dream Destination

During one of my travels, I met an author while I was waiting for connecting flight in Dallas to reach my final destination. He happened to be conducting a book-signing ceremony. When I approached to find out what his book was about, he greeted me and sounded off with, "Hi, I'm living my dream." Until I heard that author make that declaration, I used to utter that same phrase, especially during the period when I was writing and promoting one of my books, *Beyond Ordinary*.

> It takes more than catchy motivational expressions to make one's dreams come true.

It takes more than catchy motivational expressions to make one's dreams come true. Actually, it takes perseverance and creativity to live them. It takes so much more to perform a thing than to simply declare it.

According to the Law of Reflection, you must help others to obtain their dreams before you can enjoy yours. What you make happen for others, someone else will make happen for you.

Reaching the Destination of Success

I mentioned reaching my travel destination at the beginning of this segment for a reason. I could have walked to my destination, but it would have taken me weeks or months to get there; or I could have driven a car and gotten there in much less time. However, achieving my dream without the assistance of others takes significantly longer, and by the time I get there, I will more than likely be too old to enjoy it. Again, by driving to my destination, I could have reached it in a day and a half, but I would then have been too exhausted to do anything once I arrived.

There is, however, a smarter and much quicker way to reach the destination of your dreams. You must allow others to assist you in your travels. Learn to take advantage of what others have achieved, so that you can avoid many of their pitfalls en route to your success.

Helping Others, Helps You

Someone dreamed long ago of airline flight to get us to our destinations much faster and with a lot less stress. Bypassing the convenience of their dream will bring you undue cost, time, and waste of energy. Choosing to walk or drive to your destination will not spare you any expenses because you would offset any savings by the purchase of food to maintain your strength along the way of the much longer walk or the more arduous drive. Flying allows you to avoid the need to spend money on food, as you would get to your destination in hours, as opposed to days or weeks. Flying also allows you to sleep during your travels—impossible to do while driving.

Keep in mind that whenever you invest in airline flight, you are investing in a dream that someone else had long ago. While the ingenuity of their travel idea may cost a little more on the front end, you will save tremendously on the back end, as you reach your dream destination in a much shorter time. Use someone else's dream to get you to yours much faster.

I Thought Like a Champion, but I Couldn't Fight a Lick

OKAY, YOU HAVE A BUSINESS CONCEPT that you believe is not only unique but you also feel it is the best children's entertainment solution for your city. However, there is a small problem; you do not have all the necessary resources needed to give life to your dream business. You hear of all the loan programs available to help small startup business entrepreneurs like yourself. You get on this emotional high because you believe that you are the perfect candidate to borrow funds. Your credit is A-1, your monthly household expenses are in the basement, and you have money in the bank. Have you ever felt as though you were constantly running headlong into a stone wall, and all the resources you needed were just on the other side? Well, this is how it was for one couple that almost gave up.

> A person who successfully goes through tough times is himself made tougher by the experience.

Unfortunately, a person who is unwilling to pay the price for the dream in his or her heart will eventually pay the price by helping someone else who has a dream in his or her heart. This couple faced one obstacle after another, and each one of them was a worthy opponent. Family members worked hard, albeit unconsciously, to deter them from their entrepreneurial endeavors. The things their family members told them would have deterred many from their goals, but they persevered. It is one thing to receive criticism from banks and friends, but to receive unwarranted, crippling criticism from immediate family members is another thing. You must be willing to fight through the discouragement from members of your family who may possess a secret desire for you not to succeed. It is not that they really want you to fail in their hearts; it is just that they do not want to be considered wrong about your possible failure. They often say that they just do not want to see you hurt by becoming optimistic. Otherwise, they will gladly trade your experience of displeasure for their pleasure.

One day the couple called for a private consultation with me to discuss what they should do. Of course, I suggested that they continue to pursue their dream. However, I knew that they were looking for more than that. They needed revitalization, not sensationalism. I simply informed them that they would have to go alone down the path of walking through the valley of the shadow of death. Nevertheless, when they come up against the shadow, I told them, remember it is just an image. A shadow is just a deterrent, not death itself. The end result will be worth all the pain and suffering you will have to incur because the rewards will be transferred to your children when you are gone. I gave them other considerations to ponder, but my final advice to them was not to give up. A year had passed and nothing seemed to have happened where their dream was concerned. To say the least, they looked defeated. The slammed doors in their faces and the frustrations of being unfairly turned down for small loans began to wear on them and create pressure between the two of them. When they noticed what was happening, they came back to me for another meeting.

I Thought Like a Champion, but I Couldn't Fight a Lick

Their marriage was beginning to suffer even more from the sacrifices they were making, not to mention the long hours he was working. The demand on her small advertising business had increased and their children at times had to experience brief absences from their parents. I remembered during one of the consultations that he exclaimed that pursuing the business was not worth losing his wife. True, I said. But, what is it worth to live your dream? Is it worth the tears and having to make the necessary adjustments so that your family stays together and the business dream does not die? The two of you are a team that the opposition is trying to divide, conquer and destroy…and obliterate any possibility of your business coming to fruition. I said, "You are closer than you think."

How do you handle the information from a qualified source when what they are sharing with you seems to be completely erratic and insensitive to your personal dilemma? Do you continue to listen when you think they just do not understand the emotional rollercoaster you are riding? I learned that mentorship is the shortest route to success. One of the most invaluable lessons I learned from my personal mentor was that if God gives you the grace to start, He has already given you the grace to finish. A person who successfully goes through tough times is himself made tougher by the experience.

This couple eventually resolved that they would open their business with or without the bank's financial backing. Their hard work and fortitude was rewarded when a realtor informed them that someone was interested in purchasing one of their investment homes. In a crumbling economy, under the debris of home foreclosure—a treasure was discovered. They were able to use monies they had saved, leased some of the equipment, and use the money from the proceeds from the sale of one of their properties. In 2009, *FUNTASTICO* opened its doors for business and Les and Cindy Hughes became the proud owners of their dream business.

One day, Les and Cindy will be able to tell you the full uncut version of their story, which will include problems they incurred that I just did not have the space in this chapter to write. However, the dream is being lived, but it is not completely fulfilled. They learned a business lesson that will help them in their next challenge, and that is franchising their dream so that others can duplicate their success. I am sure that if you were to ask them whether their journey was easy, they would tell you that they never thought they would have to fight so hard and so long to claim a promised dream they knew was theirs. You see, if you think like a champion, you are going to have to learn how to fight like a champion too!

Can You Handle the Truth?

CAN YOU HANDLE THE TRUTH? Most people are not enthusiastic about hearing the truth, especially when it involves honest criticism about specific shortcomings. The majority of us would rather bury our heads in the sand as opposed to facing the sting of brutal, honest assessment from someone else.

As a result of this tendency, most people are apt to walk around in self-denial regarding their inadequacies or failings. To exacerbate matters, fear causes some to create parallel realities in which to bury unresolved faults. Instead of making the tough decision to confront undesired qualities, they choose, instead, to shift the blame to manufactured excuses—excuses that seek to justify substandard performance.

Henry Ford once said, "The man who believes he can and the man who believes he can't are both right." Most people have experienced

> Most people would rather hear a lie that sooths than the truth, which can be therapeutic.

money problems at one point or another in life. Yet, they do not give up on life; rather, they continue to march forward until they can either find a solution to their problem or concoct a suitable scapegoat.

Manufacturing reasons or excuses to justify an unwillingness to succeed merely exposes a person who is immobilized by fear. Oftentimes, people place God at the center of their blame, and they use Him to justify their unproductive lifestyles. In all honesty, it is very easy to find solace in our inactivity if we can connect it, somehow, to the notion that we are waiting on God to give us a clear set of instructions. And as long as we hear nothing from God, we are safer then in doing nothing. Such reasoning and rationale exposes a profound lack of self-confidence and trust in God's creative design.

Because God gave you intellectual ability, physical strength, and personal will, did He not also give you the ability to use these gifts as you deem necessary?

In just three months, you can free up sufficient cash to redirect towards paying off debt, if you can believe. Reducing your debt load begins by simply starting and reversing the same process that brought it to you in the first place. I have heard many people say, "But I don't know where to begin." My response is simple. I merely respond by asking how they amassed their debt to begin with. Generally, most respond that they fell down the slippery slope by collecting credit cards and systematically using them.

I then recommend that they simply reverse the process by desisting in their credit spending ways and then systematically paying off each credit account.

Do not be afraid to examine how you got into your financial mess. Retrace your steps and you will end up where you started—debt free.

Change is Inevitable

CHANGE IS INEVITABLE; change is perpetual; and change is powerful because all things are subject to it. Change is a powerful agent because it knows no bounds and has the ability to modify and manipulate everything in its wake. Where change is not tempered and left to its own devices, it reduces the nature of everything to its original state of dust, given enough time.

God gave man the ability to manipulate the effects of change, to either slow them down or speed them up. For instance, aging and death are inevitable, but maintaining good health slows the aging process and possibly delays death for a time. In other words, we can live at the slowest rate of death possible by maintaining good health through good diet and exercise.

> Change is a powerful agent if a person knows how to use it to their advantage.

Imagine what happens to the human body when we discard exercise and healthy eating. The body deteriorates and the rate of death accelerates. This same effect holds true in other aspects of life, including our financial matters.

Money problems do not get better if left to chance. If anything, financial troubles tend to get worse if we pay them no attention. In order to improve your situation, you are going to have to take a deliberate approach to managing your financial affairs. Ignoring debt collectors will not cause them to go away, but communicating your circumstances to them will, in most instances, relieve much stress, as they are more inclined to work with you when they understand your situation. When you face your financial challenges head-on, you neutralize the effects of bad choices that neglect brings about.

You have the ability and authority to influence change in the direction of your choosing. Therefore, make calculated improvement with respect to your financial situation. Making calls to your creditors and informing them of what you are able to do will cause them to work with you on a plan that is mutually beneficial, under the circumstances. After all, they want to recover their money, despite the fact that it may take longer than originally anticipated.

Do not be intimidated about writing down all your bills on a sheet of paper. Moreover, do not avoid any of them despite how shocked you are with the amount owed. Remember, it is not how much you owe that matters. What matters most is how much you own. Owing creates a deficit while paying off what you owe generates an asset.

Navigational Principles in a Bad Economy

In 2009, THE OBAMA ADMINISTRATION painted a very bleak picture for our nation, as he declared that the only way to jumpstart our sagging economy was for Congress to pass his $800 billion stimulus bill. However, time has proven that his estimates have fallen far short of what he and his economic advisors had hoped would be sufficient stimulus to resuscitate our ailing economy. As 2009 drew to a close, he once again looked to Congress for more bailout money.

Everywhere I travel, I find that the average Joe knows very little about the intricacies of the stimulus bill. Yet, they clamored for its swift passage. Now that Congress approved and released the bailout moneys, the President now has his sights set squarely on passing the largest health care plan in our nation's history. Is anyone concerned with where the hundreds of billions

> You are not a creature of circumstances; you are a creator of them.

of dollars are coming from to subsidize these mammoth government programs? It seems not.

Americans should be very concerned that our country is quickly sliding into a socialist abyss. The rest of the world used to observe us from across the shores in utter amazement; they continue to marvel at the amount of progress we have made in so little time, in comparison to other industrialized nations. Our free-market system is quickly becoming a relic, as our federal government acquires ownership rights in many of our largest corporations, like Citibank, Freddy Mac, and Fanny Mae. At stake are our free enterprise system and the protection of individual property rights. It will be interesting to see where we go from here.

My personal views have nothing to do with traditional party politics; I am neither a Republican nor a Democrat. I simply love this country, and I am very concerned with the current course we have chosen to pursue. The American Dream used to be a beacon of hope for millions of Americans and citizens from other countries; indeed, it lured foreigners from all nationalities to our shores. Big Brother, however, is quickly snuffing out the light that used to shine brightly. Excessive taxation is crippling our industrial might, as it did in other former great empires.

Therefore, do not allow the government or its special interest groups to decide the condition of your world. You are not a creature of circumstances; you are a creator of them. Personally, I refuse to allow fate to blow me in the direction of its choosing. I am the captain of my destiny, knowing that God has given me all the creative potential to create the kind of world in which I want to live.

You must do the following seven things if you are to navigate successfully through these uncertain times. Others have employed these principles, only to discover the benefits of having done so. The seven navigational principles are:

1. Trust God and ask for directions. (Each individual's problem is unique.)
2. Balance your bank account(s). (This will help start you at zero.)

Navigational Principles in a Bad Economy

3. Negotiate with creditors. (Even though you are not behind in your payments.)
4. Work on getting rid of high interest and long-term financing. (Exchange for short-term.)
5. Look for new ways to reduce your debt. (Abandon companies before they abandon you.)
6. Increase your giving towards God's work. (When you take care of God's business, He will take care of yours.)
7. Have faith in God's ability within you to conquer and dominate your world.

Do not allow problems to control your life, but continue to control your life while in the midst of your problems.

What is Leasing Space in Your Head?

IF YOU DO NOT LIKE WHAT YOU are watching on television, change the channel. If you hold the remote control in your hand, is it not in your power to change the channel to whatever you want to watch? Of course it is. The television station or programs you choose to view are the images that are leasing space in your brain. The same holds true for the periodicals, newspapers, and books you read. If you would honestly assess the nature of the information you pour into your brain, I am certain you would be utterly shocked at the tenants you have upstairs.

Information is the rudder that steers our lives—in the direction of its subject matter. The information we choose to believe is what programs us to behave the way we do.

> There are no fewer opportunities today than there were a year ago.

On just about every channel you turn to on television, someone is predicting doom and gloom for our economy. Little do people realize how this negative news has influenced their thinking. The negative information has infected ever aspect of our lives, from our homes to our churches, to our work environments, to our places of recreation and even to the venues where we learn. The negative talk consumes much of people's conversations.

Does anyone see an upside to our current economic condition? If so, where are their voices?

You hold the remote control to your life. Change the channel if you do not like what you are seeing. The power to do so is in your hands. Do not buy into all that negative spin going around in the media. Our economy may be reeling from the shock of one bad decision after another, but hope remains for those who have unplugged themselves from all that doomsday news.

How is it possible that some people have found ways to continue making fortunes in the midst of a severely depressed economy? The answer is simple. They decided to switch the channel from recession to progression. There are no fewer opportunities today than there were a year ago. Perhaps the tenants leasing space in your brain are not revealing to you where the opportunities are. Yet, wealth-building opportunities still abound.

Tune in to my channel, and you will discover the information that will help you locate your hidden treasures, while you learn to get your life back on track. You have nothing to lose, but a whole lot to gain.

Six Awesome Points for Greatness

As I gaze across the full spectrum of humanity, I cannot help but notice certain prominent characteristics that stand out. I encounter many people on a daily basis—many of them I run across because of their proximity to my office or in my sphere of business influence. They all share one thing. People have a tendency to wear the aura of where they have been and the influence of others. A person's actions reveal many things about where they have been and with whom they associate. It does not take long before you are able to discern the scent of a person's travels.

What do you smell like?

If a person traffics in circles where others reward or celebrate egocentrism, then he or she will tend to be self-

> People will not listen to you until you give them a reason to.

centered, as well. However, if an individual operates primarily in a very competitive atmosphere, he will approach life very competitively, more than likely. Nonetheless, I do not discern the scent on many people that would indicate that they have been in an atmosphere where others are influencing them to pursue their passion for personal growth. If a person who is a supervisor does not seek further personal growth and career advancement, those below him may soon cultivate a complacent attitude and approach to their own careers. If those employees are not careful, their boss's lack of ambition to achieve more can cause them to become stuck in go-nowhere positions. Without being aware of it, that supervisor is providing a poor example that many of his subordinates will follow.

Phil Jackson's Leadership

I am an avid sports enthusiast, and I consider myself to be an astute student of various sports—namely football, basketball, and baseball. I am particularly fond of the Los Angeles Lakers. Phil Jackson is not simply a good coach; he is widely regarded as a great coach because of the record number of championships he has won with different teams, despite always having started under very undesirable conditions. You would think that a large percentage of his players would become great players under his tutelage. In fact, most players do not adapt well to Coach Phil's system. As a result, many of them are cut from the Lakers team.

Six Protégé Points

A young basketball player may have played one or two years for the Lakers under the great Phil Jackson, but that does not make him a great player. We should never be so quick to confer the title of "great" on anyone simply because of the status of his or her mentor. Individuals must decide to embrace the teachings of a great mentor or coach. If you do, you greatly increase your chances of becoming great yourself. If you do not, you increase the odds that history will never vote you into anyone's Hall of Fame.

Great people earn great reputations. However, do not think for one minute that the great reputation of your past coach or mentor will be sufficient to allow you to escape the trial of having to prove your ability to cut it in your profession. People will not give you a pass until you first earn it. Never presume that you can use the name of some great mentor as currency to spend in a new position or on another team. People will not listen to you until you give them a reason to. Moreover, you should never attempt to have others open doors for you by dropping the name of some high-profile associate. Your actions will quickly impugn your character, if you do.

People excel under the training regimen of great leaders. Over time, they begin to develop the heart of that individual. Ultimately, what matters most is that you put into practice what you gain from those who are great.

Conclusion

Leaders, coaches and trainers eventually die and systems become obsolete, as players become bigger, stronger, wiser and more agile. In spite of this, there is One Leader and system that will never go out of style or become irrelevant, and He is the greatest leader of all time.

> "If you have really heard his voice and learned from him the truths concerning himself (Jesus), then throw off your old evil nature—the old you that was a partner in your evil ways—rotten through and through, full of lust and shame. Now your attitudes and thoughts must all be constantly changing for the better."
>
> —Ephesians 4:21–23 (TLB)

Decide today to follow His teachings!

Awakening the Seed of Potential

A FEW YEARS AGO, ARCHEOLOGISTS found a 4,000-year-old Egyptian mummy. They were amazed to discover several seeds of wheat that the mummy clutched tightly in its hand. Although the mummified body had withered significantly, the seeds remained intact with the potential still inside to produce a wheat harvest. If you were to plant any one of those seeds in fertile soil, you and I would be able to enjoy the results of what someone harvested 4,000 years ago. Scientist estimate that if just one of those wheat seeds continued through the normal cyclical reproductive growth patterns over a twenty year period, it would yield the equivalent of the annual wheat harvest of the entire world.

> Unrealized potential is a tragic indictment against the one who possesses it.

Instead, the seeds lay inert for 4,000 years. Secure in the mummified hand, they could not fulfill their God-ordained purpose—reproduction after their kind.

Unexpected Treasures

Unrealized potential is a tragic indictment against the one who possesses it. It forever lives as a legacy of what might have been. The potential that you and I never harvest dies to history as a major catastrophic disappointment.

As with the seeds in the hands of the 4,000-year-old mummy, the potential for success is in your hands. However, there is no guarantee that you will ever discover yours. Success always begins in seed form, and the power of the seed is only realized when you sow it in the earth. The dry seeds of your potential are in your possession, but they are currently dormant. To stir them from their slumber, you need only to feed them the vital nutrients of your loving time and passionate attention.

The coat of any seed feels like leather and it looks like plastic. It is designed to protect the seed from humidity and dirt while it sleeps. When you water it, amazing things begin to happen. Scientists still do not fully understand the miracle of life that issues forth from something as simple as a small seed. Witnessing a seed wake from a dormant state is an awesome thing to behold.

No less awe-inspiring are you when you awake from your slumber. When you begin to tap into your potential, you will notice that your dreams and aspirations will begin to unfold before your eyes. Imagining all the things you can accomplish is amazing, but actually experiencing them is far better.

Do not allow the seed of your potential to go to the grave without first watering and harvesting it. To live and not reach your potential is to live…not at all.

The Value of Experience

EXPERIENCE IS EXPENSIVE TO ACQUIRE, and the lessons of life never end. Just when you think you have graduated from the school of experience, along comes a completely new study course, complete with end-of-course final exams. Have you ever felt that you would sign up for more classes in experience if the tuition were not so costly?

There is a great deal of value tucked inside every life experience, but extracting the value is a steeper price than most people are willing to pay. Our experiences oftentimes cost us more later in life because of our unwillingness to pay a much cheaper present value. In all actuality, experience is vital because it prevents us from repeating bad mistakes—at least it should. If you continue to revisit similar bad experiences, it means you did not pay attention in class.

> Avoiding your weaknesses will not cause them to disappear.

Life is full of problems and diverse struggles. Your challenge is to gain as much understanding from your experiences as possible, so that you journey through them without coming out smelling like smoke.

Unexpected Treasures

What Greek Mythology Can Teach You

From Greek mythology, we get the tale of the invincible Achilles who, as a baby, was dipped into special water that would make him immortal and render him impervious to injury of any sort—except on both of his heels, where his mother held him for immersion in the river Styx. Because the water did not touch Achilles' heels, they were the only two vulnerable points on his body. In one particular battle, an arrow mortally wounded Achilles when it pierced one of his heels. Down through the many centuries since Homer first introduced us to Achilles in his tale, *The Iliad,* we have come to refer to a person's weaknesses or vulnerabilities metaphorically as his or her *Achilles' heel*—that seemingly very small but unprotected area in a person's life that has the potential to destroy him.

Weaknesses and Vulnerabilities

All of us have weak and vulnerable areas of our lives that we struggle with. When problems come our way, our tendency is to fix our focus on what we can see instead of what is not visible. Most people choose to treat the symptoms of their problems rather than the actual root cause, because the source of the problem often entails working on one's self. We are quick to conclude that 'me' is not the problem; the problem is 'you.'

Avoiding your weaknesses will not cause them to disappear. If you choose to avoid your problems, you will remain unprepared for life. As a result, you will acquire many Achilles' heels. Life is loaded with difficult struggles. If you are going to get through the struggles of life, you are going to have to struggle to get through. You cannot afford to remain passive in the face of the very problems that seek to take you out. I discovered long ago that life is not a dress rehearsal; it is the actual stage production. People experience real-life divorce, rape and incest, death, financial ruin, and myriad other devastating tragedies.

The Value of Experience

Making Adjustments

When you are experiencing turbulence in your life, you must learn to make timely adjustments and turn the autopilot switch to the off position, so that you can gain control. With sober thought, you must read the instrument panels to determine the proper course of action you need to take according to the storms that blow in your direction. As you ride out each storm, you will gain confidence, and you will rid yourself of every Achilles' heel that has the potential to level you.

To succeed in life, you must hammer out your weaknesses, confront your fears, and persevere in the midst of opposition…until you get through every storm on your horizon.

Remember the immortal words of Booker T. Washington…

> "Success is to be measured not so much by the position that one has reached in life as by the obstacles which he has overcome while trying to succeed."

Excuse Me, Can I Order Success Here?

IMAGINE THE HEADLINES: "Success Pills Sold Here! Lady Swallowed Success Pill and Won the State Lottery!" Unfortunately, success does not grow on trees, it cannot be purchased at your local supermarket, nor can one dig it up as though it were lost treasure. SUCCESS...this most sought after commodity, has never lost its appeal, and everyone seems to be chasing it—especially in America. How important is success to you? What price are you willing to pay for the kind of success you desire? For some people, success is so important that they are willing to exchange their dignity for it. What an exorbitant price to pay for something we can all gain with just a little extra effort. Imagine the risks people take just to obtain such a bounty. It is not wrong to desire success. In fact, it is intertwined within your DNA to be successful and/or to work hard to accomplish your goals.

> Become a success where you are and you will be successful where you are going.

Why is success so important to so many people, and why is it viewed as a prerequisite to a fulfilled life? One explanation can be advanced by determining what defines you as a person. If success is the ultimate defining essence of your being, then this is why you will do anything for it. I believe that success is important because by it, a person gauges their final status and effort. To complete a particular task is an indication that one is successful. Success is the efficient accomplishment of a goal. To reach the expected end is an accomplishment; it is being successful.

Success at Any Cost?

Is attaining success worth compromising your integrity, by cheating on a test or lying to your supervisor in order to mask your real reason for tardiness? If you were to accidently destroy company property, would you hide the fact and hope that someone else takes the blame? Would you receive the accolades from others for a job you never performed, instead of giving credit to whom it is due? All the aforementioned illustrations demonstrate an obvious lack of integrity and a breech in one's character. Is this success or pretense?

The "Working Girl" Success Example

I am reminded of a movie called, "Working Girl." This movie is about a secretary who had a knack for acquisitions, but she worked for a female boss who arrogantly dismissed her suggestions merely because she was a secretary. One day her boss went to Aspen, Colorado on a ski vacation, and during one of her ski runs, she broke her leg. As a result of the accident, her doctor advised her to remain in Aspen for several weeks until she was capable of air travel. Her secretary viewed this unfortunate situation as an opportunity to research a large company that could possibly purchase a number of failing radio stations. It ended with the owner of the large company loving the idea, and so he wanted to go over the particulars.

Meanwhile, her boss came back and discovered that her secretary was about to secure a deal that she herself was ill-prepared to sell, because she had no concept of how her secretary came up with the figures. Yet, her boss somehow was able to convince the owner that she created the concept and that her secretary stole it from her. However, when she was unable to answer the questions the owner posed, he figured out that she was lying. The truth prevailed and the wealthy owner hired the secretary as one of his assistants and gave her an office with a window and a secretary of her own.

Success Achieved!

This person found success even though she was a lowly secretary. She simply wanted the opportunity to grow and use her ideas to do what had always been in her to do. The secretary was held back by a witchy, insecure boss who could not see that she was already successful without having to step on others to achieve it. Be a success where you are and you will be successful at where you are going. Always give credit to whom credit is due!

Living By Your Convictions

THERE ARE TIMES WHEN PREFERENCE has to take a back seat to conviction. These are the times when what you choose is not necessarily your preferred choice, but it is the best choice for you. A person cannot continue to live their life in the shadow of maturity or else their future will be crammed with ineffective decisions and vacant dreams. When you sleep at night, is it your heart or your brain renting space inside your dreams? Are your dreams overflowing with personal desires because you lacked things as a child, or are they inundated with the mandate in your heart to accomplish a purpose that involves you and a great many others?

> Conviction will see your dreams through, but preference will keep them in a holding pattern.

The Art of Conviction

Parents should learn to master the art of conviction. Most parents know this principle all too well because when a child is born, the child's needs take precedence over the parent's wants. Unfortunately, far too many parents have yet to adopt this principle as a standard; therefore, their children are left in the hands of a cruel world.

Wisdom vs. Irresponsibility

In life you will always be forced to decide between things you want to do and things you have to do! Choosing correctly between the two ever-present options is the difference between wisdom and irresponsibility. Wisdom will provide balance to your decision-making and keep you from making impetuous decisions that lean heavily on gratifying your wants. For instance, a man believes that working long hours to provide for his family is the most prudent course of action for him to pursue, based on his passion for his work and his conviction for taking care of his family. While his convictions may be heartfelt, carrying them out may actually run counter to what is best for his family overall. While his heart is to provide for his family, spending excessive hours at work may mean that he misses quality time with his wife and children, a dynamic that can ultimately put a strain on family relationships.

Resolving the Dilemma

Wisdom will cause a person to weigh the two options and resolve the dilemma appropriately. Both the need to fulfill the demands of work and the requirement to raise one's children are equally important. How do you do both when you cannot be in two places at one time? This is a valid consideration. However, the solution is time management. Loving your family enough to provide for them is very noble because this is a quality missing in the American culture, but it is never a substitute for spending time with them. Quality time is more important than the quantity of time.

Conviction Will Manifest Your Dreams

Conviction over preference drives a person to overcome their fears and inhibitions to convert substance of their dream into present reality. You may not have an intimate knowledge of how every detail of your

Living By Your Convictions

dream—business, financial situation, or life circumstances—is going to turn out, but somehow you just believe that they will materialize exactly as you envisioned them. You are fully aware that the prelude to accomplishing your dreams will be marked by days when you go without your Starbucks coffee, or you miss your favorite television program, or when you simply have to press harder just to get through discouragement. Being convinced of what is in your heart to achieve is clearly evidenced and demonstrated by what gets done. Conviction will see your dreams through, but preference will keep them in a holding pattern.

I Planted Corn, but I Expected Wheat

I ONCE HEARD A PREGNANT TEENAGER say to her parents while crying and talking about her condition, "I didn't think I would get pregnant. We only had sex once." Scientists understand that the entire universe is established based upon laws that govern the present status, the outcome, and the potential modification of any particular thing. And, these laws are irrefutable and immutable; the law of Sowing and Reaping is one of them.

A Seed Reproduces Itself

Perhaps one of the most insidious mistakes one can make is to believe that

> The seed of money is money.

you do not reap what you sow...but what you think you sow, what you say you sow, what you wish you had sown, or what you want others to believe you have sown. Nevertheless, realize that you reap what you have actually sown. How ridiculous it would be for a farmer to plant a field full of wheat and then expect to reap corn at harvest time. Would he receive corn instead of wheat merely because he inadvertently planted the wrong crop, or because he wished he had planted corn, or because he told his neighbors he had planted corn? Of course not! He would reap what he had sown. So it is with you and me. If we deceive ourselves, even innocently, or deceive others, perhaps intentionally, it makes no difference. Whether you believe this or not, your spiritual crop will be faithful to your actions, not your intentions.

It's not Luck; it's Reciprocity

People generally do not like to hear the truth about why they are in a financial mess, but the truth must be grasped if change for the better is going to occur. The final error of reasoning that leads us to believe we do not reap what we sow is the belief that we humans are mere victims of circumstances—that our lives are the result of mere luck. Not true. The young pregnant girl at the start of this chapter did not become pregnant because of some freak accident. She became pregnant because she had unprotected sex. The effect of this false belief can easily be seen in a problem experienced by millions of people worldwide—global obesity. It seems incredible that only one cookie, one piece of cake, or one extra soft drink could make so much difference. So we go blindly on, adding cookies to cake to soft drinks until our waistlines reap the fruit of our illogical thinking.

It's Universal

The law of Sowing and Reaping applies to our financial status, marriage, how we raise our children or oftentimes how we are treated by others. Our status did not develop into what it is without someone first determining what it would be. If you waste your time complaining about never having enough money, your brain will never have the time to create new ways to increase your income. If money is time and time is money, then wasting time is wasting money.

Making it Work for You

This particular law of Sowing and Reaping is not a law for Christians and entrepreneurs only; it is a universal law that affects every person and thing on Earth. The law of gravity does not affect one segment of the population; gravity affects everyone. If you jump from a twenty-story window onto concrete, there will be an expected end: self-destruction. If you have worked at something for three to five years and it has produced little or sporadic income, then allow your creative juices to flow in order to attract more money.

When a person is interested in changing what his or her life produces, they will have to learn how to develop a mentality to attract the things they desire to adorn their life. Learn how to attract money instead of working for it. You are a magnet that attracts what you are and how you believe. In some cases, you may have mastered a strong belief, but you believe in the wrong things. Change what you believe and your results will be different. Make sowing and reaping work for you instead of against you.

I Thought
I Was in Hawaii...
69

WHAT DO YOU DO WHEN after you get up in the morning and the kids are yelling at one another, you are behind on a couple of bills, you're running late for a business meeting, your spouse and teenagers don't get along, your money is funny, the toddler's hungry, you have a doctor's appointment later that afternoon for your uncontrollable cough, your phone continues to ring, your parents are ill, your siblings are depending on you for moral support during their personal crises and the list goes on? Well, what do you do?

> Life happens to everyone!

1. Do you scream I want out of here?
2. Do you imagine yourself in Hawaii? Or
3. Do you go through the Yellow Pages to find the nearest psychiatrist?

If your answer is all of the above, you are correct if you are like most people. However, you are not like everyone who whimpers under the daily pressures of life.

Functionally Depressed People

Most people in this case become functionally depressed. They are capable of functioning during the course of the day, but they are seriously facing depression that can move for the better or it can get worse. The one thing that needs to be understood is that everyone, at one time or another, experiences some form of depression. A slight case of depression is not the end of the world. In fact, it is the start of a new world that is drastically being altered by your present mental status.

It's All in Your Head

You see, your mind controls your world. It is not the circumstances that one goes through that changes their world; it is how their mind perceives the situation that makes their world what it is. On the other hand, there is nothing wrong with wanting to leave for Hawaii in the midst of turmoil.

We have all wished that we were somewhere else when our circumstances seem to have gotten the better of us. However, if you mentally escape for hours in your make-believe trip then I might say that you are leaning toward a nervous breakdown. Get help as quick as possible from a qualified source. Your mind is trying to find ways to cope with what it is experiencing because there may be little or no attempt on your part to take control of your situation.

Coping with Life

Although there is no single cause for depression, we are aware that one factor is psychosocial. Psychosocial is relating to both the psychological and the social aspects of something, or relating to something that has both of these aspects. To put it plainly, it is how your mind copes with the problems you experience. Life happens to everyone! During your days on God's green Earth, you are going to have problems—it is a part of life.

I Thought I Was in Hawaii…

Commanding Your Mountains

Instead of allowing your circumstances to leave an impression of depression, turn them into an aggression of expression. Meaning this: Control the outcome instead of allowing the chips to fall where they may. Napoleon Hill once said,

> *"Every adversity, every failure, every heartache carries with it the seed of an equal or greater benefit."*

The problems we incur in life would not be considered hurdles or obstacles if there was no way over or around them. There are no hopeless situations; there are just people who have grown weary as a result of them. Make a conscious decision that you will not allow your once-in-a-while problems to result in everyday feelings of depression. Give firm instructions to the disorder in your life, and it will follow your command. When your molehills turn into mountains, do not look at the size of them and consider how you are going to climb them. Jesus once said to His followers,

> *"You can say to this mountain, be removed…and it will obey you."*

Therefore, command your mountains! It takes too much time to climb them.

They Said Walt Disney Had No Imagination

HAVE YOU EVER WONDERED what comprises the crucial difference in the way people respond to life's challenges? A major segment of the world's population has been bathed in frail attempts that are inundated with half-hearted efforts. No one ever truly succeeds by trying. Somehow, the word 'try' gives me a vivid picture of a rope attached to it, leading back to the comfort zone of mediocrity. To try something is an uncommitted or reluctant approach to accomplish one's objective. If a person is committed to their dream or family or business pursuits, they will cut themselves off from all sources of retreat—leaving them with one option, to win. When a person has an unwavering devotion to a belief in their heart, even if they fail time after time, they will continue to get up and resume their unwavering devotion to their belief.

> Apathy is the enemy of achievement and the antagonist of pursuit.

Bankrupt

Walt Disney was fired by a newspaper editor because the editor felt "he lacked imagination and had no good ideas." Several times, he went through bankruptcy before he built Disneyland. In fact, the proposed park was initially rejected by the city of Anaheim because they felt that it would only attract people of low social status.

They Told Sidney Poitier to Wash Dishes

The first African American Academy Award Winner for Best Actor, Sidney Poitier, was told after his first audition by the casting director, "Why don't you stop wasting people's time and go out and become a dishwasher or something?" It was at that moment, recalls Poitier, that he decided to devote his life to acting.

A World of Difference

There is all the difference in the world between the expectations of the person who has committed him or herself to their life's purpose without reservation, no matter the sacrifice, having vowed to see his or her aspiration to the end, and the person that goes about his or her objective halfheartedly. Apathy is the enemy of achievement and the antagonist of pursuit.

The Challenge of Failure

Failure usually affects people in one of two ways: It serves as a challenge to greater effort, or it subdues and discourages a person from trying again. How a person reacts to circumstances reveals both the brilliance and intensity of their drive or the lack thereof. Obstacles and challenges are not what relegates a person to poverty; their mindset is what places them in the prison of hopelessness. Many people accept their lot as inescapable and go through life wearing dispossession as a shackle.

Rising Above the Hardships

I realize that in times past, African Americans, American Indians and Hispanics have been systematically excluded from and/or allowed only limited participation in the American Dream. Yet there are many who have achieved wealth and educational status despite the efforts of some Americans to prevent these accomplishments from happening. Obstacles and opposition are a part of life; and millions of Americans had better get used to it. I am convinced that the chains of mental slavery and the segregation from the success of living ones dreams is arguably the most horrendous transgression any person can confer on oneself. Fortunately, since this mental incarceration is self-induced, the solution to these barriers lies within our power to free ourselves.

> The solution to these barriers lies within our power to free ourselves.

Conclusion

God gave you the power to create the framework of your life by the way you think and believe; but He also gave you the power to change it.

Turning Stress Into Strength

MY LIFE WAS ON THE BRINK of destruction and no one knew it but me. I experienced a near brush with a real-life mental meltdown and I hid so well that I successfully hid it from myself. Over one-hundred and fifty million people suffer from one form of depression or another. People have a tendency to look at their leaders, parents, teachers, clergy, spouses and even politicians and assume that they are strong and will always be strong, despite the circumstances. Unfortunately, oftentimes this is not how it turns out.

> If stress is not controlled, it graduates into depression.

The Commonality of "Blue Funk"

Depression is a common experience today. We have all felt 'depressed' about a misunderstanding in our marriage, altercations with teenage children, a cold shoulder from a friend. Sometimes we feel 'down' for no reason at all. Depression does not always start as an illness; it usually begins as a depressive thought or mood. However, depression can become an illness when your mood state is severe; when it interferes with your ability to function at home or work, or when your state of mind lasts for more than two to three weeks.

The Weight of My Fortieth Year

My personal clash with my depressive state started with a multi-million dollar building program. If I did not know the devil was real, I sure discovered how real he was during this ordeal. It was 1998 and I was just turning forty. Turning forty was not the problem; I could easily cope with this. The problem was that the first building contractor embezzled approximately $300,000 at the outset of our building project. Because of this action, the bank refused to continue funding the project pending the outcome of our litigation proceedings. At times, I would cry uncontrollably and for the life of me could not figure out why. I ended up in the hospital being examined for chest pains only to discover that I was suffering from chronic stress and depression. After my escape from the hospital, I had no other choice but to get back into the thick of things. Winston Churchill made frequent references to his depression, which he called his "black dog". Churchill knew that during World War II, not only was his nation depending on his decision-making ability, but other nations were as well.

Crying After Winning

In order for the bank to continue funding our new construction, we had to win our lawsuit. While sitting in court, after the judge adjourned, I found myself crying as everyone else was leaving the courtroom. Surely, I was much stronger this, I thought to myself. After finally winning the court case, the bank continued to fund our project and we resumed construction. Two weeks later, our 130 × 55 foot-high wall was twice blown down by a strong wind. It was at this point I realized I had simply resolved in my heart and mind that the things I cannot control, God can and what I can control, I will.

Stress Can Lead to Depression

My temporary depressive state was brought on by a high degree of stress, which I had to learn to use to my advantage, not my demise. Stress is an unfortunate, unpleasant fact. However, possessing a healthy sense of control—a confidence in your ability to influence the course and destiny of your life—can help you manage stress by shortening its duration or avoiding it altogether. If stress is not controlled, it graduates into depression. The signs of being in a depressed mood are lowered self-esteem, insomnia or broken sleep, less ability to control emotions from pessimism to anxiety, changes in weight, and an absence of or reduced sex drive, etc.

Real People Overcoming Real Problems

Having one or another of these symptoms, by themselves, is unlikely to indicate depression. However, there could be other causes that may warrant medical assessment. I do not claim to be a licensed clinical psychiatrist; I am just a real person who has experienced real problems, and I have discovered how to combat them and win. Reduce stress and you will lengthen your life.

> I have learned how not to sweat the small stuff.

Two Types of Stress

There are some things you can do to help reduce stress in your life regardless of the situation. First, I believe that you should understand stress to some degree. There are two sides to stress: One is when confronted by a threat to its physical well-being, the body undergoes what is known as the stress response. It temporarily abandons its long term "building projects"—growth, tissue repair, immune function, etc. Instead, it floods the bloodstream with glucose, protein and fat from reserves in the liver and fat cells. Heart rate, blood pressure and breathing rate skyrocket. These physiological changes can save your life by giving you extra speed, strength or a more focused mind. The other side is that the stress response occurs not only when we are confronted by physical danger, but also in situations that simply make us feel anxious—from getting stuck in traffic to an argument with your spouse or co-worker.

Small Things That Lead to Victory

I discovered little things that helped me to turn stress into strength and here are a few of them. Reports say that people who have a connection with God and involvement in church have a health advantage. Determine that you are a person who acts, and does not always react. Calmly do these things:

- Be proactive
- Develop a positive interaction with your family
- Take advantage of certain outlets
- Talk positive
- Avoid perfectionism
- Stretch your facial muscles with laughter. (Humor extends life)
- Diversify your life
- Enjoy periodic massages
- Stop assuming the worst
- Leave your work at the job
- Read Dr. Mikel Brown's books (Smile)
- Relax and focus your thoughts

Research has discovered that 'attitude' toward oneself and the environment is the key to managing stress. Therefore, enjoy the "now", remain in the moment, and release your mind from built-up concerns and tensions. **DON'T WORRY! BE HAPPY!**

72

The Power of NOW

ARE YOU NEXT, LAST OR NOW? If you ever played pick-up basketball in the gym or at the neighborhood playground, you are very familiar with these words: "I got next!" You cannot say this phrase passively because during the course of a game, the noise could be intense and the focus of everyone around the basketball court is on the teams playing at that moment. Your tone has to be demanding and your presence without intimidation, or else someone will claim your spot and go next. The problem with being next is that "next" may never come.

Choose to be First

There are times when people have the option to be first but they choose to be last in hope that it would prove to

> Think Big!
> Think NOW!

be the best choice. I can recall a football game that went into overtime. When the referee tossed the coin, the team that won the toss chose to kick off to the opposing team. Now allow me to expound on how this overtime ordeal works in football. In simple English, the first to score, wins. Why would you reduce your chances of winning the football game by kicking off to the opposing team when you could be the receiving team and increase your chances of winning? What was going on in the mind of the coach that won the toss? Is last a great position? The result was that the team that won the coin toss lost the game because the opposing team scored first.

Forget Next! Think Now!

There is another posture that should be taken into consideration, and that is the NOW mind-set. The word "now" means at the present moment, currently, at once, or in that instant. The person that is in the game usually is better off than the ones who are waiting to be next or last. I do not believe that Bill Gates saw his company as the next IBM or Michael Dell saw his firm as the next Apple Computer. These men demonstrated a resilience to be proactive in their pursuit of providing a quality product. Who would want his or her company to be a carbon copy of someone else's dream? If this is your desire, to mimic something already in existence without improving on it, then your ideal is just a cheap copy of a great original. Are you the next big thing? See yourself as the BIG thing. Think Big! Think NOW!

> Prepare your future NOW by getting every tool you will need to accomplish every goal you have in order to custom-design your tomorrow, today!

Preparing Your Future

Inspiration is in the details. If you are meticulous about your future and you do not trust your future in the hands of others, then you have to take control of the helm and not let go. Your vision will succeed because of your strong and active attribute to seize the moment. Refuse to entertain thoughts of being next or last when you are there now. Define your unique vision of success and do not just be in the game of life and business, dominate it. Never stop learning, growing, building, and strengthening your forces. Experience the magic of bonding with dynamic, determined, well-seasoned people who will help expand your spirit and your resources. Prepare your future NOW by getting every tool you will need to accomplish every goal you have in order to custom-design your tomorrow, today!

See Yourself There

See yourself in the moment. You are not getting there, you are there. You are in the fast lane without the thought of getting out of it until your objective is accomplished. You represent your definition of excellence, not someone else's. The game is not over as long as you are in the game.

About The Author

This book is like having a life and business coach right in the palm of your hand. Inside the covers of this book are theapeutic anecdotes and professional recommendations that can empower you and make a difference in the quality of life you choose to live. What is it that makes the difference in the quality of people's lives? What shapes your ability to contribute to your success or failure? Personal appreciation and fulfillment from helping someone other than you, is exactly what Dr. Mikel Brown has mastered. The people who have weathered some of the most horrific experiences have found away to become one of those persons who contribute the most to society. Dr. Brown always says contribute beyond your need. Dr. Mikel Brown was born in the fifties during the mid-civil rights movement.

Raised part of his life in Cabrini Green Projects in Chicago during the sixties and later moved to predominately-white suburbia on the South Side of Chicago in 1968; he has seen his life go from one extreme to the next. While being the only black family in his Chicago Southside neighborhood, young Mikel endured extreme prejudice. He could have made the choice to become bitter, but he decided to become better. Excuses are claims to your missing resources and they stifle your creativity to be resourceful. When the obvious is a fact, facts are subject to change. Two negatives will simply short-circuit your power, but if you combine the positive and the negative—what you have is a release of power. You become empowered to live life to its fullest. "Your life is not short of resources… you lack the knowledge to be resourceful," says Dr. Brown. Your treasures are neatly stored and compiled in one of the most unexpected places—you!

Index

57 Varieties, 139

Abbot, Jim, 3
abilities
    innate, 38
    potential and, 17–18
abundance, mindset of, 144
Achilles, 180
addictions, as learned behaviors, 117–18
adversity. *See* challenges.
age, 29–31
American Dream
    future of, 168
    minorities and, 201
apathy, 200
appearance, external, 79–81
attitude
    changing one's, 143–4
    control over, 99–100, 136
    formation of, 143–4
    NOW mindset and, 207–9
    stress management and, 206
    tenacity and, 57
    See also beliefs *and* thought.

bailouts, financial, 167
Ball, Lucile, 16
Beethoven, Ludwig Van, 2
beliefs
    circumstances determined by, 137–8, 193, 196–7, 201
    commitment and, 199, 201
    firmness of, 142
    See also attitude, mindset *and* thought.
Beyond Ordinary, 144, 157
Biggest Loser, The, 50
brain, sophistication of, 150
Brown, Debra, 42–3
Bryant, Kobe, 53
Building Wealth from the Ground Up, 92

challenges
    meeting, 47–50, 58–9, 61–2, 78, 97–8, 132, 159–62, 181, 197, 199
    personal growth and, 127–9, 152, 179–81
champion inside you, 113–16
change-adeptness, 39, 165–6

character, importance of, 38
Charles, Ray, 3
Churchill, Winston, 3, 204
cockiness, 5–6
comfort zone, dangers of, 114–15
commitment, power of, 199–201
composure, maintaining, 7
confidence
    necessity of, 100,
    low, 148, 164
conscious mind, 142
control
    exercising, 91–2
    sense of, 205
convictions
    achieving success and, 184–5
    preferences vs., 187–9
counting your blessings, 126
Crawford, Fred, 122–3
creditors, negotiating with, 166, 169
criticism
    dealing with, 160
    honest, 163
Curves fitness centers, 30–1

David (king of Israel), 38
Davis, Sammy, Jr., 3
debt
    Americans and, 91
    freedom from, 93–4, 164, 166, 169
    obligation to pay, 21–3
Dell, Michael, 208
depression
    causes of, 196, 205
    functional, 196–7
    resisting, 135–6
    stress and, 205
    widespread, 203–4
Disney, Walt, 200
divorce
    causes of, 133–4
    recovering from, 121–3
    See also marriage.
Dream Makers 99 conclaves, 29, 71
dysfunction, 85–7

economic crisis
    future of America and, 167–8
    upsides of, 172
Edison, Thomas, 2
education, relative value of, 83–4
Einstein, Albert, 3
emotions, as learned responses, 125–6
endurance, 51–2
excuses, 9–10
experience, learning from, 179–81

Faber, Katelyn, 53
failures, overcoming, 54
failures
    success and, 114
    learning from, 152
    response to, 200
    See also challenges.
faith
    necessity of, 141–2
    See also belief.
father figures, mentorship and, 13–14
fear
    as excuse, 9–10, 77–8, 163–4
    facing, 181
    overcoming, 77–8, 153, 181
finances. *See* money.

Index

'first things first' principle, 114, 117–19
focus, maintaining, 6–7, 18–19, 58
followers, leaders and, 156
follow-through, 14
Ford, Henry, 139–40, 163
free-market system, future of, 168
fulfillment
    jobs and, 147
    service to other and, 106
    success and, 104
functional depression, 196–7.
Funtastico, 161

gambling addiction, 92
Gates, Bill, 208
General Motors, 38–9
giving to God, 169
goals
    after reaching, 152, 157–8
    consistent effort and, 151–2
    motivation and, 153–4
    setting, 109
    vision and, 56
God
    blaming, 164
    dependence on, 136
    focus on, 12
    giving to, 169
    intends success for us, 140
    life's purpose and, 14, 89–90
    serving, 106–5
    trust in, 164, 168–9
Goldberg, Whoopi, 3
Gore, Al, 118
Graham, Stephen, 10
greed, 35

habits, formation of, 117–19
happiness, false sources of, 11–12
healthcare reform, 167–8
Heinz, Henry J., 139–40
help
    from others, 158
    need to ask for, 63–4
helping others, 158
Hill, Napoleon, 99, 197
honest, about self, 101–2
How to Fix Your Marriage without Using a Hammer, 134
Hughes, Cindy, 161–2
Hughes, Les, 159–2

IBM, 39
impulse spending, 21–3
influence of others, 173–4
information
    external sources of, 137–8, 171–2
    negative, 171–2
insecurity, 150
integrity, achieving success and, 184–5
introspection, 134, 143
irresponsibility, wisdom vs., 188

Jackson, Phil, 174
Jesus Christ
    following the teachings of, 175
    on overcoming obstacles
    on prayer, 142
    on service to others, 107
jobs, attitudes toward, 147–8
Jones, James Earl, 3
Jordan, Michael, 1–2
Joshua, 16

judgment, withholding, 53–4

Keller, Helen, 2
Kentucky Fried Chicken, 30

Law of First Things, 114, 117–19
Law of Reflection, 26, 157
Law of Sowing and Reaping and, 191–3
Law of Starting and Finishing, 145–6
leaders
    followers and, 156
    reputation of, 174–5
    vision and, 56
leadership, Phil Jackson and, 174–5
learning, necessity of, 13–14
legacy, life, 111–12
limitations, self-imposed, 137–8
listening, learning and, 14
Lombardi, Vince, 118
Los Angeles Lakers, 174
love of money, 84
love of neighbor, 102
love of self, 102
luck, relying on, 16

Mandela, Nelson, 52
marriage
    causes of failure of, 133–4
    dysfunction in, 86–7
    healthy, 134
    See also divorce.
maturity, perseverance and, 61–2
Maynard, Kyle, x, 2
mental toughness, cultivating, 5–7
mentorship, 13–14, 64, 161, 174
middle class, money and, 34

Millionaire Wealth-Building Strategies conclave, 71
mind, potential of human, 149–50. *See also* mindset, beliefs *and* thought.
mindset
    changing one's, 143–4
    control over, 99–100, 136
    formation of, 143–4
    NOW mindset and, 207–9
    stress management and, 206
    tenacity and, 57
    See also beliefs *and* thought.
minorities, American Dream and, 201
misfortune, overcoming, 49–50. *See also* obstacles.
Model T, 139
money
    attitude toward, 33–6
    belief and, 142
    Christian view of, 84
    fulfillment and, 106–7
    law of Sowing and Reaping and, 192–3
    love of, 84
    no "secret" to success with, 103–4
    purpose of, 95–6
    slavery to, 106
    success and, 104
    wasted, 96
    See also money management.
moneymakers, world shapers vs., 105–7
money management
    attitude and, 33–6
    deliberate approach to, 166

Index

"hidden" money and, 95–6
See also money.
mothers, influence on children, 43–5
motivation
    finding, 37–40, 153–4
    reasons for, 154
multi-tasking, focus and, 19

negativity, turning away from, 171–2
Nelson, Turnel, 112
New Year's resolutions, 151–2
NOW mindset, 207–9

Obama, Barack, 167
obstacles
    overcoming, 47–50, 58–9, 61–2, 78, 97–8, 132, 159–62, 181, 197, 199
    personal growth and, 127–9, 152, 179–81
occupations, jobs as, 147
'Our Great Fear,' 81

Parable of the Pencil, 73–5
parents, convictions of, 187–9
passions
    key to success, 109–10
    motivation and, 154
    pursuing, 18, 104, 109–10
past
    escape from, 154
    learning from, 111–12
    overcoming, 52
Paul (Apostle), 84, 106
perseverance, 52, 57–9, 61–2, 132, 145–6, 152

planning, success and, 141–2
Poitier, Sydney, 200
poor class, money and, 34
potential
    of human mind, 149–50
    reaching, 17–19, 51
    talent and, 17–18, 38
    unrealized, 177–8
prayer, need for, 142
preferences, convictions vs., 187–9
principles
    importance of, 86
    success and, 103–4
    See also standards.
priorities
    alignment with, 11–12, 19, 107
    'first things first' principle and, 114, 117–19
    life's purpose and, 12, 14
problems, dealing diligently with, 16
procrastination, 65–7, 78
Proctor, G., 29–31
psychosocial causes of depression, 196
public schools, low standards of, 51–2
purpose, life's
    priorities and, 12, 14
    total commitment to, 200
    understanding, 136

Reflection, Law of, 26, 157
repetition, learning and, 142
reputation, earning, 174–5
rhythm of life, 11–12
risk, aversion to, 84

risk, necessity of, 62
Roosevelt, Franklin D., 3
Rudolph, Wilma, 3

sales, credibility and, 101–2
Sanders, Colonel, 30
scarcity, mindset of, 144
self-confidence
    low, 148, 164
    necessity of, 100,
self-doubt, mastering, 113
self-esteem, building, 25–7, 79–81
    low, 148
self-imposed limitations, 137–8
self-knowledge, 101–2
self-love, 102
self-motivation
    finding, 37–40, 153–4
    reasons for, 154
selflessness, 156
serving God, 106–7
serving others, 106–7
Sherman, William Tecumseh, 48
silent followers, 156
Sowing and Reaping, Law of, 191–3
spending, compulsive, 21–3
standards, setting high, 51, 86–7
Starting and Finishing, law of, 145–6
stimulus bill, 167
strengths, weaknesses and, 115–6
stress
    cause of depression, 205
    kinds of, 205–6
    managing, 206
subconscious mind, 142
success
    academics and, 84
    belief and, 142
    choosing, 70–1
    failures and, 114
    'first things' principle and, 118
    God's intention for us, 140
    fulfillment and, 104
    importance of, 183
    integrity and, 184–5
    measuring, 109
    money and, 104
    no secret to, 103–4
    passion and, 109–10
    planning for, 141–2
    potential for, 178
    principles and, 103–4
    true nature of, 103
Sylvia's Restaurant, 131–2

talent
    vs. potential, 17–18, 38
    work aligned with, 148
teachability, 13–14
teamwork, effective, 155–6
tenacity, developing, 52, 57–9, 61–2, 132, 145–6, 152
Thoreau, Henry David, 97
thought
    action and, 26–7
    changing patterns of, 119
    controlling, 171–2
    See also beliefs *and* mindset.
Tillis, Mel, 3
time management, 67
trying, ineffectiveness of, 199

uncertainty, 149–50
uniqueness, 69–7

Index

value proposition, personal, 69
vision, necessity of, 55–6
vocations, jobs as, 147
vulnerabilities. See weaknesses.

Walker, C.J., 41–2
Washington, Booker T., 42, 181
weaknesses
    facing up to, 180–1
    knowledge of, 115–6
    personal growth and, 127–9
wealth
    attitude toward, 33–6
    belief and, 142
    Christian view of, 84
    fulfillment and, 106–7
    law of Sowing and Reaping and, 192–3
    love of, 84
    no "secret" to success with, 103–4
    purpose of, 95–6
    slavery to, 106
    success and, 104
    wasted, 96
    See also money management.

wealthy class, money and, 34
weight loss, 50
White, E.B., 16
Williamson, Marianne, 81
Winfrey, Oprah, 43
wisdom, decision making and, 188
women, unique virtues of, 41, 43–5
Wonder, Stevie, 3
Woods, Sylvia, 131–2
Woodson, Carter G., 27
Working Girl, 184–5
world shapers, moneymakers vs., 105–7